HOW TO
LABEL A GOAT

THE SILLY RULES AND

REGULATIONS THAT ARE

STRANGLING BRITAIN

ROSS CLARK

Hh

Harriman House Ltd
43 Chapel Street
Petersfield
Hampshire
GU32 3DY

Tel. +44 (0)1730 233870
Fax +44(0)1730 233880
Email: enquiries@harriman-house.com
Website: www.harriman-house.com

First published in Great Britain in 2006 by Harriman House Ltd.
Copyright © Harriman House Ltd

ISBN 1-897-59795-9
ISBN13 978-1-897597-95-8

British Library Cataloguing in Publication Data
A CIP catalogue record for this book can be obtained from the
British Library

Printed and bound by Biddles.

About the author

Ross Clark is a journalist who has written extensively for *The Times*, *The Sunday Telegraph* and *The Mail on Sunday*. For some years he wrote a column in *The Spectator* entitled 'Banned Waggon' which exposed, week by week, the Government's obsession with stopping us doing things. He also writes a regular column for *Real Business Magazine*, looking at the impact of regulation on business.

He is also the author of *The Great Before*, a satire on the anti-globalisation movement – www.greatbefore.com.

Contents

I

HOW TO
LABEL A GOAT

*"And he shall set the sheep on his right hand,
but the goats on the left."*
St Matthew 26.33

IN just 16 words the Lord separated the sheep from the goats. If only the National Assembly of Wales could be so succinct. But sadly not. On 4 April 2006 it passed the Sheep and Goats (Records, Identification and Movement) (Wales) Order 2006, regulating the size, shape and colour of ear tags on Welsh sheep and goats. It ran to 45 pages.

For anyone unfamiliar with this text, here is a taster (I quote the English version by the way, which I suspect may have been translated from the Welsh original):

Subject to sub-paragraph(2), when a keeper moves an animal from any holding (other than the holding of birth, holding of import or holding of identification) to temporary grazing and returns that animal from temporary grazing directly to the holding, he or she must:

(a) attach a movement tag to that animal when it leaves the holding;

(b) enter the movement tag code in his or her register when the animal leaves and when it returns;

(c) enter the movement tag code in the movement document that accompanies the animal when it leaves the holding; and

(d) enter the movement tag code in the movement document that accompanies the animal when it returns from temporary grazing to the holding unless the animal is tended by a different keeper of temporary grazing, in which case that keeper must complete the movement document in accordance with sub-paragraph 3(b)

With no disrespect to Welsh hill sheep farmers, who are a fine body of men, I just wonder how many are really educated to a standard which enables them to decipher 45 pages of densely-written legalistic language, or indeed make any kind of sense of the above paragraph. And if they can, how many really want to be bothered going through the kind of rigmarole described above every time they want to move their sheep to that slightly greener pasture down the hill. We have reached the bizarre situation where hill sheep farmers have to keep sheaves and sheaves of records on the life history of every scraggy sheep – and yet where the Home Office manages to lose track of 1,000 convicted foreign murderers, rapists and robbers who should have been, but weren't, deported upon finishing their prison sentences.

It is not that the Sheep and Goats (Records, Identification and Movement) (Wales) Order 2006 is anything unusual. I picked it out to begin this book because I was particularly struck by the images conjured up by one sentence buried deep in the 45 pages of legislation. It begins: "*If an animal is already marked with three eartags…*"

One pictures herds of these poor beasts lumbering about the Welsh hills, dragging their ears along the ground behind them, beladen with multi-coloured tags – just to please the bureaucrats in Cardiff.

There were plenty of other examples of over-bearing or simply lunatic rules and regulations which I could have used to begin this book. Where to start? In the 12 months to 31 May 2006 the Government passed 3,621 separate pieces of legislation. Yes, that is more than 10 new sets of rules and regulations for each day of the year. To give an idea of the sheer weight of these regulations I sampled 10 per cent of the Government's regulatory output for the 12 months to 31 May 2006, counted the pages and then factored them up. It came to a shocking figure: 72,400 pages of legislation and 26,200 pages of explanatory notes – a total of 98,600 pages of official bumf.

That is equivalent to *War and Peace*, 70 times over. It is a hundred thousand American Declarations of Independence. If the pages were laid out end to end they would stretch for 18 miles. If piled on top of each other the documents would reach the height of a London bus – or rather they would have done had the London bus not itself been the victim of health and safety regulations. It is an ironic footnote that London buses, banned because somebody might possibly fall off the open deck at the back, were replaced with 'bendy buses' which mysteriously started bursting into flames, sometimes

with passengers inside them. But then that so often is the story with health and safety legislation…

Just how do MPs find time to plough through all this legislation before voting on it, you may wonder? The answer is they don't. The vast majority of new laws and regulations are not passed by act of parliament: they are 'statutory instruments' – direct edicts, in other words, of the Government and its numerous agencies. Indeed, the 3,621 pieces of legislation in the 12 months to 31 May 2006 break down into 29 acts of parliament and 3,592 'statutory instruments' – essentially new laws which have been passed without reference to our democratically-elected representatives.

Any society needs laws and regulations, but if it has reached the stage at which our elected representatives don't know what is going on, how are the rest of us supposed to know? While there have always been silly laws and red tape, the past few years have witnessed an acceleration like never before. Like some unhinged robot in search of suppressing its human masters, the regulatory machine seems to be feeding upon itself. And you and I, not to mention our schools, hospitals, factories, offices, pleasure parks and just about everything else, are paying the price.

Just how does the Government manage to come up with nearly 100,000 pages of regulations? A few, no doubt, are necessary. But just to give a flavour of the regulatory overload which has become endemic, take this example from the 157 page Clean Neighbourhood and Environment Act 2005 which came into force on 6 April 2006.

The act empowers local authorities to deal with the problem of abandoned shopping trolleys which disfigure our streets and parks. To anyone not employed in local government this may seem a straightforward enough task: you ring up the shop and tell them that one of their trolleys is lying on its side in the allotments off Brook Road and will they please come and pick it up. If they don't, you send it to the crusher.

Ah, but that is not nearly tidy enough an answer for the bureaucratic mind. Before a local authority can dispose of a single shopping trolley it must now first devise a shopping trolley policy. To do this it must:

Consult with "all local retailers who offer a trolley service", with representative bodies such as the British Retail Consortium, the Association of Town Centre Management and the Association of Convenience Stores, and with other businesses and landowners, local residents and community groups, the Police and the local chamber of commerce.

Once the local authority has done this it may proceed to make a resolution on abandoned shopping trolleys and publish notice of this resolution in at least one local newspaper.

After three weeks have elapsed the council is then able to implement its new abandoned trolley removal policy, but subject to the following conditions:

1. Before any trolley can be removed permission must be sought from the occupier of the land where the trolley was found abandoned. If permission is not forthcoming the local authority may serve notice on the occupier stating that it wishes to recover the trolley. If no notice of objection is received within 14 days, the local authority may then proceed to remove the trolley.

2. The local authority must then store the trolley for six weeks, during which time it may be claimed by the owner. In the first 14 days of this period a notice must be served on the shop which appears to be the owner of the trolley. If the owner comes forward, the local authority must then deliver the trolley to the owner. In return for doing this it may then recover the costs of transport, administration costs and storage. The shop may, however, appeal against these costs if it can prove that it was not the owner of the trolley at the time it was found abandoned.

3. Finally, following implementation of the trolley removal policy it must then review the policy every five years,

in the meantime taking care to monitor the number of trolleys which have been recovered under the policy, and whether the policy is having an impact on the rate of trolley-abandonment.

No wonder council tax bills have doubled in nine years, and that the public sector payroll has swelled by over 500,000 in nine years with little discernible improvement in public services. If there has been an epidemic of abandoned trolleys it is probably because Government ministers have fallen off them.

It goes without saying that the 98,600 pages of new legislation come at a price. According to the Better Regulation Taskforce, which was set up by the Government to fight red tape, regulation costs Britain £100 billion per year, 12 per cent of GDP and more than the yield of VAT and fuel duty together. And that is the Government's own figure.

I'll take their word for it. It is very nice of ministers to come up with a figure informing us of just how much their footling bureaucracy is costing us. But one wonders how many bean-counters were employed to calculate it, and just how much they cost us. Bean-counting, indeed, has become one of the country's fastest-growing industries.

To take but one bizarre example of the art:

In the year 2005/06 the Royal Cornwall Hospitals Trust found itself £8 million in debt. It blamed its shortfall on an obscure bureaucratic formula by which the NHS granted it less money per patient than comparable hospitals in the Home Counties – the argument being that the cost of living is lower in Cornwall and therefore it should cost less to run a hospital. This might well be the case were it not that the Royal Cornish Hospitals Trust is bound by law to pay its doctors and nurses the same national pay scales as a hospital in, say, Surrey.

Mind you, the Cornish hospitals could save a bit of public money by cutting back on one bizarre bureaucratic procedure of its own: it has ordered nurses to conduct a 'chocolate audit' of its wards. Bewildered staff were ordered to count up the number of choccies – and other gifts – donated by grateful patients so that the information might be used to help construct an index of patient satisfaction. At the end of the year the Trust was delighted to announce that patients had made 8,000 'grateful gestures' – compared with writing only 316 letters of complaint.

One suspects that this rather crude measure will be only the beginning. After all, it would appear to value a humble box of Roses as equal to a large box of Belgian truffles.

Should boxes of chocolates not be graded according to their size and luxury, so that NHS bureaucrats are able to build a more precise picture of the levels of patient – sorry, consumer – satisfaction? Don't worry, the new improved choccie index will soon be on its way – unless, that is, the health and safety police have first dreamed up a pretext for banning chocolates from NHS wards altogether.

No doubt the Cornish hospital's choccie index will be one of the pieces of information entered onto the NHS' new supercomputer when – or rather if – it ever sees the light of day. The National Programme for IT, the Department of Health recently admitted, could end up costing taxpayers £20 billion.

And to what purpose? Did patients never get treated before the advent of supercomputers? Of course they did. In fact, one might well argue they got treated rather better in the days when hospital staff were employed primarily to look after patients rather than to gather data. The £20 billion computer system is a symptom of what is going wrong, how the bureaucratic way of doing things has come to infect just about every area of national life.

For this book I have gathered some of the most amusing, lunatic or just plain sad stories of bureaucratic overload I could find. A word of warning: it might make you sick. If nothing else, you might feel faintly nauseated by the realisation that while the Government has foisted 98,600 pages of legislation upon us, many of its rules do not appear to apply to itself. Take sex discrimination legislation, which was found in court to render Labour's women-only shortlists illegal. Did Labour change its rules on women-only shortlists? Like hell it did. Rather, it simply changed the law. It is now illegal to discriminate on the grounds of sex when

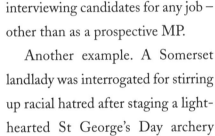

interviewing candidates for any job – other than as a prospective MP.

Another example. A Somerset landlady was interrogated for stirring up racial hatred after staging a light-hearted St George's Day archery competition in her pub – which involved firing arrows at the dragon on a Welsh flag. It was a different story, naturally, when the Prime Minister was reported for inciting racial hatred after the former deputy head of Downing Street communications accused him of referring to the "F***ing Welsh" when it seemed the dastardly country was going to reject his plans for a Welsh assembly. Downing Street expressed incredulity that the Government's own laws on racial discrimination should apply to the Prime Minister himself. After a brief investigation police dropped the whole business.

Why wasn't the Prime Minister cautioned – like a London street-trader arrested for behaviour which 'may cause alarm or distress'. His crime? Displaying a tee-shirt with the words: "Bollocks to Blair".

It is a thread which runs through this book: the petty rules and regulations which press down on the rest of us but from which, by one means or another, our leaders have managed to excuse themselves. Take the ban of political advertising on television and radio, introduced by the Communications Act 2003. It prevents us buying advertising space to campaign to save our local hospital or to protest against Government foreign policy. Yet does it prohibit party political broadcasts by the main parties? Er, no. Or take the employment laws which oblige any company wanting to rid itself of incompetent employees to leap through four or five hoops before it can formally hand out the P45s. Does that apply to the Prime Minister when he wants to sack political renegades from Government jobs? Er, no, he simply lifts the phone and fires them on the spot.

As for John Prescott who is, at the time of writing, still notionally deputy prime minister in spite of conducting an affair with an aide in his office: can he really be a senior member of the same Government which passed legislation making it an offence to ask a job applicant an innocent question about her family, on the grounds that it could constitute discrimination?

I only ask.

2

I CAN'T

HONESTLY SAY

IT IS A NEW

PHENOMENON...

TAKING part in my first nativity play at the age of five, there was something gnawing away at the inside of my skull. It was the explanation as to why Mary and Joseph, she heavily pregnant, had to travel 80 miles on a donkey from Nazareth to Bethlehem. St Luke explains it thus:

"And it came to pass in those days, that there went out a decree from Caesar Augustus, that all the world should be taxed. And all went to be taxed, every one into his own city."

Why the hell couldn't they have put the cheque in the post? Or at least Caesar Augustus might have put one of his tax-collectors on the road. But to send every man, woman and child back to their home town just for the privilege of being taxed? Come on, even Her Majesty's Revenue and Customs doesn't force me to make an annual trip to Worcester – where I was born – to pay my taxes (though on second thoughts it would probably be quicker than filling in a self-assessment tax return, and if the cricket was on it would make a nice day out).

So much for the supposedly efficient Roman way of doing things. The more one thinks about it, the more the tax system in first century Judea comes across as either a) a means of drumming-up business for inn-keepers, donkey salesmen or both; b) a chronic lack of planning; or c) sheer bloody-mindedness. Perhaps it was a mixture of all three.

I raise this issue because it is important to make the point that, however maddening we find bureaucracy in an advanced industrial nation, it is far from being entirely a modern phenomenon. To take but one example, for sheer verbosity and enthusiasm few current-day pen-pushers could compete with the Treasury staff who composed the Land Tax Act 1791. It consumed 780 skins of parchment, running to 1,170 foot in length.

The desire to regulate is as old as the human race itself. I am sure that, given time, archaeologists will be able to uncover ancient statutes governing the size and depth of tread of early stone age wheels; that a tablet of stone will be uncovered at Stonehenge detailing the regulations governing the construction of henges; that amid the ruins of Pompeii will one day be found, etched in a hundred pages of papyrus, the detailed risk assessment for the continued habitation of the city – and that this will run something like: "Though there is a chance of further volcanic activity at Mount

Vesuvius, it is considered to be minor in nature and as such constitutes little risk to the people of Pompeii, providing the correct procedures are followed regarding the proofing of buildings against the incursion of ash."

What is different about the present day, of course, is the advent of the computer. While they are jolly useful machines for many purposes, improving productivity and automating many previously tedious tasks, they have provided almost limitless possibilities for Government targets. When forms – theoretically at least – can be handled automatically, the quantity of documentation which a Government feels it can unleash upon the population is able to expand exponentially.

Equally important, perhaps, is the supply of white collar labour. State bureaucracy could not have attained the gargantuan proportions which it has without the ready availability of willing bureaucrats. In pre-industrial times, the proportion of people whom a society could spare for clerical tasks was necessarily very low: most hands were needed in the fields. Agricultural improvement freed workers from the fields, who were then mopped up by the factories. Rationalisation of industry, and the switch of production to the lower wage environment of the third world freed labour to be sucked into the great service economy of the 1980s, memorably described by one cynic as a world in which 'we all sell burgers to each other'.

But what happens when the sale of burgers is rationalised to the point that there are not enough service jobs to keep everyone busy? There is then only one place for surplus labour to go: into public administration, telling people how they can and can't serve their burgers. Since 1997 the Government has created half a million new public sector jobs. That it has done so is largely a reaction to the demand for administrative work. The typical college graduate had great-grandparents who worked upon the land, grandparents who worked in factories, parents who sold shoes from the boot of a Ford Cortina – and who, armed with three years of further education, has the opportunity to progress one step further up the socio-economic ladder: as an 'officer' in some Government quango. You can wear a suit and tie, and you don't have to go out in the cold and wet. You get a nice pension and the chance to feel jolly important.

In a sense, excessive bureaucracy is an inevitable result of progress. We can be thankful that we live in a society so rich and secure that it can spare the labour for meaningless public sector jobs such as 'diversity officer', 'anti-social behaviour outreach worker' and, my personal favourite, Head of Barking Enterprises (a £60,000 a year job supposedly encouraging job-creation in Barking, East London). Nevertheless, it is hard to feel a pang of regret that we are not still back in the days when bureaucrats had to chisel out their documents by hand...

A BRIEF HISTORY OF RED TAPE

3rd millenium BC: World's first urban civilisation emerges in Mesopotamia with 3rd dynasty of Ur. And with it comes the world's first petty bureaucracy. More than 2,400 stone tablets have been uncovered, most of which, historians admit they have not yet bothered to read. To give you a taster: one of them records all the movements of sacrificial sheep and goats during the 8th year of Amar-Suen's reign. No wonder counting sheep has become a byword for going to sleep.

1057: Lady Godiva wins a notable battle against the petty taxes imposed by her husband Leofric, Earl of Mercia. She is appalled that the burden of paying taxes leaves the populace with no time to engage in the arts. He agrees to rescind most of the levies on Coventry's citizens if she will agree to ride naked through the marketplace. She does it and the taxes are removed (admittedly, along with Leofric's plans to provide the town with a fresh water supply). What chance Cherie Blair following Lady Godiva's example? No, on second thoughts, I would rather pay the tax.

1086: William of Normandy kicks off the modern obsession with bean-counting by ordering the Domesday Book, registering every eel, cottage and head of cattle in England. Over 900 years later, when Edgar's three ploughs in Lower Poopington have long since been replaced by Land Rover Discoveries, I am still at a loss to know why he wanted the information – which, after all, would have already been out of date by the time it was inscribed on parchment.

1215: Magna Carta signed by King John – as some would have it – to enshrine our liberties in law. Those of bureaucratic mind celebrate it more for the passage which heralds the arrival of the weights and measures man: "There shall be one measure of wine, ale and corn (the London Quarter) throughout the Realm. There shall also be a standard width of dyed cloth, russet and haberject, that is two ells with the selvedges. As it is of measures so it shall be of weights."

1314: First record of petty-minded legislation: Edward II issues a royal proclamation banning football in London.

1414: First British passport issued. No record survives of how long the applicant had to queue, nor whether the Passport Office bought him an umbrella while he waited in the rain.

1604: James I invents the nanny state by banning the import of tobacco, describing smoking as "a custom loathsome to the eye, hatefull to the Nose, harmful to the braine, dangerous to the Lung, and in the blacke stinking fume thereof, nearest resembling the horrible stygian smoke of the pit that is bottomlesse." At least the language is more evocative than 'smoking causes fatal diseases'.

9 January 1799: Perhaps disappointed by revenues from the hair-powder tax, introduced in 1795, William Pitt the Younger subjects the British people to income tax for the first time, with a rate of 10 per cent for incomes of more than £200 a year. All was explained in the succinctly-titled leaflet: A Plain, Short and Easy Description of the Different Clauses in the Income Tax so as to render it familiar to the Meanest Capacity. The leaflet caused such horror that all copies were destroyed when income tax was – temporarily – abolished three years later.

1835: Government bean-counters cause their greatest mayhem yet. Houses of Parliament burn down when a fire of old tally sticks discarded by the Exchequer gets out of hand.

1 July 1837: The Government dreams up the idea of registering the existence of every human being born in Britain. Little could the parents of Mary Ann Aaron of Dewsbury, Yorkshire, the first baby to be registered, have guessed that it would lead to the Government holding data on our irises, and ethnic origin and even whether we prefer the vegetarian option when we fly to America.

TO CYCLISTS! THIS HILL IS DANGEROUS

1879: First piece of idiots' advice appears on a sign on a steep hill outside Scarborough: "To cyclists: this hill is dangerous". It leads to a fine tradition of fatuous advice, including the labels on peanut packets warning: "may contain nuts" and a sign spotted on the mirror of a motorcycle on sale in the US: "Warning: objects seen in the mirror will be behind you".

1992: Ken Clarke confesses that he has never read the whole of the Maastricht Treaty, the document which John Major's government has staked its reputation on ratifying in the British Parliament. This establishes the principle that Parliament is merely a place to rubber-stamp legislation made by bureaucrats elsewhere, without even bothering to find out what it says.

1 May 1997: Tony Blair and New Labour elected. There follows the creation of half a million new public sector jobs, but strangely public services barely improve. Could it be that all these extra officials are merely getting in the way?

The rest, as they say, is history. Let's leave William of Normandy and Edward II behind and have a look at the weird and wonderful achievements of Britain's modern day officialdom.

3

NO TAXATION

WITHOUT

COMPLICATION

E VERY April I look forward to what for me, and just about everyone else who runs a business or is self-employed, has become something of a rite of spring: filling in my tax return. I know I am a little unusual – even perverse in this – but I actually enjoy it. I love its language. At first sight a tax return is banal. But the more one ploughs through its many pages, supplementary pages, notes, guidance and help sheets, the more it takes on a surreal air. It is a parallel universe where one minute you are filling in details of your granny bonds; the next you are suddenly whisked away to an exotic world where you are being accused of international money laundering.

In particular, I enjoy nothing so much as the moment, in help sheet IR35 when, after a drill on the intricacies of National Insurance Contributions, one is suddenly asked the question, apropos nothing:

Are you a deep-sea diver?

I am not. In fact the closest I have ever got to diving was

when, aged nine, I bor-
rowed my brother's
facemask and
snorkel, and fumbled
around in the shal-
lows off Margate to
retrieve the corpse of
a recently-departed
starfish. But it still
intrigues me as to
why the Inland
Revenue feel the
need to ask. Have I
not just spent sev-
eral hours filling in forms to the effect that I am journalist?
What likelihood then that midway through my tax return I
have decided to retrain as a diver?

The more one thinks about it, the more bizarre it seems.
Even if I was a deep-sea diver, why should it make any difference to the tax I pay? Admittedly, deep-sea divers have a pretty
dangerous and often unpleasant job. They run the risk of the
bends and being gobbled by a giant clam. But then one expects
their pay to reflect that. I cannot for the life of me see why the
taxman should seek to create a special tax band for divers.

And what about scuba divers? Do they have a different tax rate still? Can they claim a snorkel reduction or a flipper allowance? And if so at what depth of sea does the deep sea diver tax rate kick in? I can almost imagine my diving instructor as I take to the deep for my first dive. "Watch out. There's a wreck at three hundred feet. And there's a gully to the north where the sharks like to hang out. But whatever you do, don't you slip over that continental shelf. You'll find yourself going down and down into the deep. And you know what that means: an extra three-fifty quid in tax next year."

It isn't just divers. I love the question in the tax return: "do you want to use farmer's averaging?" It sounds like a euphemism for the poor grasp of mathematics among rural folk: if you are a farmer and you are having problems with the maths on your tax return, don't worry – just use 'farmer's averaging' and take a wild guess. Actually, it is a device allowing farmers to iron out the ups and downs in their income – similar in fact to the follow-up question: "do you want to use 'literary and artistic spreading?'", which sounds like an expression for the expanding girth which writers and artists are apt to acquire while confined to their garrets. But don't other businesses suffer from seasonal variations in their trade? If farmers and artists can average their income of several years for tax purposes, why can't we all do this?

Gordon Brown, the longest-serving Chancellor of the Exchequer of the past hundred years, has made an art out of complicating the tax system. Taxation has become so complicated in recent years that Tolleys, the privately-published bible of tax advice, has doubled in size in recent years and now paginates at a formidable 850 pages. The writers of that guide, believe it or not, are masters of brevity. Her Majesty's Revenue and Customs (HMRC) can't boil their own regulations down with anything like Tollys level of concision.

In 2005 the accountants KPMG – commissioned, it has to be said, by a Government concerned about the complexity of tax regulation – conducted a study into the weight of tax regulations weighing down on British business. Businesses, they found, are potentially liable to fill in a total of 279 different tax forms, and supply a bewildering total of 6,614 different pieces of information.

Needless to say, supplying the information is not quick – or easy. The total cost to British business of complying with tax regulation, KPMG's bean-counters went on to calculate, is an astonishing £5.1 billion a year. And that is just the tax system – it excludes the cost of complying with such things as health and safety, environmental and planning law. Moreover, it excludes the millions of man hours spent by individuals filling out their personal tax returns.

The business of paying tax has become so complicated that even the professionals cannot get it right: according to HM Revenue and Customs four out of ten corporation tax returns filed in the past year have contained errors – and they are mostly audited by top-notch accountancy firms, staffed by people with years of training.

If trained accountants can't cope with tax returns, what hope the ordinary individual? Until the mid 1990s, filling in the tax return was a relatively simple business: you were asked for details of income from various sources, you filled in a brief form and the taxman did the rest. Then came 'self-assessment': a wonderful scheme whereby the number-crunching once done by the taxman would instead be done by you and I – via a 'tax calculation guide' which runs to 16 pages and requires 131 separate calculations to be made. Theoretically, one might have expected this huge transfer of effort to have been accompanied by a rapid reduction in the number of employees at the Inland Revenue. Yet strangely this does not appear to have happened.

What are all these pen-pushers supposed to do with their time? Other, that is, than sending a Lincolnshire taxpayer a bill for four pence, with the words: "this does not have to be paid immediately, though interest will be added." Simple: they are administering – or rather trying to administer – the fiendishly complicated world of tax credits. 'Tax credits' – effectively means-tested state handouts by another name, paid to the less well-off – which in practice means any family earning up to £60,000. You pay the taxman with one hand, and, if you meet the right criteria of neediness, he gives you some of your money back. The Government's argument for tax credits is that they enable the Chancellor to target particular groups of people with financial help: for example pensioners and families with young children. It is argued that a more obvious form of help for the low paid – cutting taxes – would not allow the Government to target needy groups in the same way.

However, an astonishing amount of the money the Government is supposed to be paying to targeted groups is not actually being paid to them. According to the Inland Revenue's own research £2.9 billion of tax credits a year is going unclaimed. A survey conducted by Age Concern revealed that a third of pensioners entitled to pension credit do not claim it, and 11 per cent of them have never even heard of the benefit. There is a very simple reason for this: the people upon whom the tax credits are targeted do not understand the forms which they are supposed to complete in order to claim them.

The only people who do seem to have mastered the forms required to claim tax credits are organised criminals. In 2006 HM Revenue and Customs admitted that 10.6 per cent of the annual £13.5 billion budget for tax credits in the year 2003/04 was claimed fraudulently. Some of the fraud had even been perpetrated under the guise of the civil servants administering the system: 10,000 civil servants were recently found to have had their identities stolen by gangs fraudulently trying to claim tax credits.

If the Government really wants to help the less well-off, as opposed to organised criminal gangs, there does seem to be an obvious solution: why not simply cut taxes, in particular by raising the threshold at which income tax must be paid, lifting tens of thousands of low-earners out of tax altogether and saving a fortune on bureaucracy?

It is, of course, too obvious a solution. And besides, what would the poor taxmen do for employment? The administration of pension credit alone employs 18,000 staff: all of whom, when they retire, will be rewarded with generous final salary pension schemes – paying rather more than the miserly £105.45 a week with which pensioners are rewarded for taking the trouble to fill out the tortuous form.

British manufacturing industry has declined markedly in recent years. Agriculture hasn't been doing so well. But fortunately we will never have rising unemployment so long as tax-collecting remains one of the fastest-growing industries in the country. Here are a few reasons why:

• On 6 April 2006, or 'A' day as it was widely trailed, the Government's 'new simplified rules' on pensions came into effect, 'offering simpler and more flexible retirement arrangements'. The changes were so complicated that businessmen had to be invited to seminars in order to have them explained. The manual explaining the changes ran to 1,369 pages.

• The London congestion charge, introduced on 17 February 2003, has, according to Transport for London, reduced the amount of traffic entering the centre of the city by 18 per cent. The same might have been achieved by employing a team of police marksmen around the perimeter roads trained to shoot out the tyres of vehicles attempting to enter. It would certainly have been a lot cheaper. Before congestion-charging was introduced, it was expected to consume £85 billion of the £185 billion raised annually in fees. In the event, the costs of the scheme, which included setting up a call centre in Coventry, were far higher. During the first six months of operation the costs of running the congestion charge swallowed 67p out of every £1 raised. Were all taxes to be constituted on the same basis, tax-collecting would easily be the nation's biggest industry, accounting for 27 per cent of GDP.

• Out of every pound paid out in income support, 11 pence finds its way into the pockets of the civil servants employed to administer it. For housing benefit the figure is 15 pence. But they are both a picture of efficiency compared with the Government's Financial Assistance Scheme, set up in 2004 to compensate pensioners who have been left penniless when their company pension schemes collapsed. In its first two years of operation, the scheme paid out a grand total of £100,000, shared between 32 pensioners. Yet in those two years the scheme cost £5.2 million to administer. Needless to say the scheme was run by civil servants who had no fear of ending up victims of a collapsed pension scheme themselves: they are all signed up on final salary pension schemes, generously underwritten by the taxpayer.

• The civil service requires the public each year to fill in a total of 1.2 billion forms: that is 20 for every man, woman and child in the country. We wouldn't need quite so many if it were not for the fact that the benefit claimants are forced to fill in four separate forms to claim working families tax credit, income support, housing benefit and council tax benefit – in spite of the fact that the forms demand almost exactly the same information.

At least British taxpayers are spared the gobbledegook put out by the Australian Taxations Office, which in 2005 was given a 'golden bull' award by the Plain English Campaign for the following extract from one of its forms:

> For the purpose of making a declaration under this Subdivision, the Commissioner may:
>
> a) treat a particular event that actually happened as not having happened; and
> b) treat a particular event that did not actually happen as having happened and, if appropriate, treat the event as:
>
> i) having happened at a particular time; and
> ii) having involved particular action by a particular entity; and
>
> c) treat a particular event that actually happened as:
>
> i) having happened at a time different from the time it actually happened; or
> ii) having involved particular action by a particular entity (whether or not the event actually involved any action by that entity).

And just to be fair to the taxman…

No-one should forget that banks can be just as absurd. A Yorkshire man received a letter from the Halifax warning him grimly:

"Your payment to your credit card account of £0:01 has not been received. If something has happened which makes payment difficult please telephone the above number"

At which point, presumably, he would have been given the opportunity to pay the outstanding balance – in instalments.

4

CARING

TO DEATH

"In a few weeks we will be sending out a customer satisfaction questionnaire. Please let us know whether there are any questions you would like to be included on the form"
County Council letter (why didn't it just ask for any comments?)

My nine year old daughter, Eliza, is mentally-handicapped. For children like Eliza, our local authority has instigated a 'link family' scheme, whereby families will volunteer to look after disabled and handicapped children, to allow the child's parents some respite. It is a lovely idea, and one which in theory should involve minimal cost to the authority. But that, of course, is to overlook the provisions of the Children's Act, which ensure that any time we save changing incontinence pads – and more besides – is instead consumed filling in forms.

Clearly, local authorities ought to guard against the possibility of handing over children into the arms of child-molesters. But, having held countless meetings and completed numerous forms ourselves I did rather despair the day that an officer from the Commission for Social Care Inspection, which I have learned regulates the link family scheme, produced a 12 page form for Eliza herself to fill in. Here is a taster of one of the 50 questions:

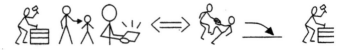

Eliza has a mental age of around three. She can read the 'E' in her name, but has not as yet learned to read whole words. But when she does, hopefully, learn to read words and sentences, I suspect that it will still be some years before she learns to understand the above question. Indeed, by the time she can read it, she will not be going off to a link family. She will be catching the train every morning to a high-powered job at the British Museum deciphering Egyptian hieroglyphics.

I have tried to work out the meaning of the above, and this is the best I can come up with:

If someone bangs your finger with a hammer, pokes you in the eye and hits your thumb with a wooden spoon you can pay them back by kicking them in the groin, throwing them on the floor and banging their thumb with a hammer.

Anyone got any better ideas? (Okay, this is what the above drawing is supposed to mean: Do you get enough help to do things?)

There is no area of national life so overwhelmed with bureaucracy as healthcare and social services. Let's start with a few figures:

• Between 2000 and 2004 the number of NHS administrative staff increased from 159,141 to 211,690. Talk about chiefs and Indians: the NHS now has 2000 non-executive directors, along with 121,505 senior managers and managers.

• There are 42 quangos working in the healthcare sector alone – or at least there were when the former health secretary John Reid promised to prune them in an efficiency drive. Among the achievements of this drive was the abolition of something called the NHS Modernisation Agency and its replacement with, er, the Health and Social Care Information Agency. A great breakthrough for the manufacturers of headed stationery, but it isn't altogether obvious how replacing one quango with another makes for efficiency.

In spite of all these managers and quangos committed to modernisation and efficiency, the NHS in 2005/06 was flushed with £81 billion of taxpayers' cash, yet still ended up with a deficit of £500 million

It is very easy to gather statistics on the NHS, and it is

nice to have them. As with all statistics, they can be used to prove virtually anything you want them to. For Government ministers this invariably means reeling off pages of figures in the House of Commons about knee operations in an attempt to fool us into thinking how jolly well the health service is doing – when the anecdotal evidence about granny's long wait for a botched knee operation is probably a better guide.

But in a way the statistics are part of the problem. They do not, after all, fall out of thin air. They exist because an army of bureaucrats has assembled them. In many cases the gathering of the statistics merely distorts the provision of the healthcare. For example, one of the Government's proudest boasts is that 98 per cent of accident and emergency patients are now seen within four hours of admission. Never mind that four hours is a long time to spend with a throbbing head or a bleeding leg, 98 per cent sounds a very impressive sort of a number and we are all supposed to feel grateful. Yet the reality is often that patients approaching the end of their four hour wait are simply wheeled along to a 'clinical assessment unit' – i.e. a corridor – next to the A&E department so that they can continue their wait there.

Ninety-eight per cent, by the way, seems to be a pretty standard figure for NHS trusts achieving their targets. In

2004 the Government also reported that 98 per cent of patients were seeing their GP within two days of ringing to make an appointment. That was all very well until it was revealed that NHS trusts had tipped off GPs practices as to when a survey was to be conducted – enabling the GPs to hire extra doctors, or locums, and so fiddle the figures.

Not that it is always in a hospital's interests to fulfil its Government targets in any case. The bizarre Alice in Wonderland world that is the NHS' internal market can mean they end up being penalised for doing exactly what the Government says it wants them to do. Doctors and nurses at Ipswich Hospital – or rather Ipswich Hospital's NHS Trust as it is officially called nowadays – worked so efficiently that they managed to cut the waiting time to see a consultant down to just a week. The result? They were docked £2.5million in funding. When a patient goes to the hospital his visit is paid for by something called a Primary Care Trust. In this case it had decided that to save money it would only pay for patients who had waited for at least 122 days. In other words, the hospital's consultants were supposed to sit around twiddling their thumbs while their patients waited for the mandatory four months waiting time had passed. It is beyond satire: vast sums are paid employing managers to shift around artificial sums of money in this bogus 'market'

– while real medical staff are mothballed.

The expression 'caring profession' sums up an ideal: it is all about working on the front line with people, rather than sitting in an office. Except that to care for people these days seems to consist mostly of filling in forms about them. One owner of a Leicestershire care home, who had been looking after old people quite blamelessly for years was sent a 28 page questionnaire by the National Care Standards Commission, which she was supposed to fill in prior to an inspection.

"It asked me for details of 40 written policies and procedures on everything from racial harassment to smoking and use of alcohol," she says. "One of the questions was whether I had a policy on 'sexuality and relationships'."

Most of the residents in her home, she adds, are suffering from dementia. They are quite unlikely to engage in passionate new relationships. On the other hand, some patients go in as married couples, having spent half a century sharing a home and a bed. One thing they do appreciate is being able to continue to share a room in their last years. Unfortunately, this is not always possible. Why not? Because the Care Standards Act 2000 insists that homes – for no discernible reason other than some civil servants thought it a good idea – must have at least eight single rooms for every double room.

The Care Standards Act 2000 promised to improve the quality of life for elderly people in residential care. The reality is that it has achieved exactly the opposite. Hundreds of homes have closed because they have been unable to match the pedantic new rules, which, for example, insist that each patient must have at least 14.1 square metres of room. Needless to say, the result of the closures was that at one point 5,000 elderly people were marooned in NHS hospital beds – beds desperately needed for other purposes – because no care home beds could be found for them.

But it wasn't just care homes which fell under the Care Standards Act. In the early 1980s a family from Oldham replied to an advert pleading for foster parents to help look after a teenage girl, Janet, with cerebral palsy who at that point had spent her entire life on the children's ward at the town's general hospital, receiving very few visitors. They took the girl home and integrated her into their family life. All was well for 20 years until the Care Standards Act came into force. Suddenly, the family realised to their horror, their home was no longer to be classified as a family home but as a care home. They were sent a form designed for a 60 bed nursing home, and informed that in future they must write to the National Care Standards Commission every time Janet contracted a cold. Moreover, as carers the family were suddenly expected to have passed National Vocational Qualifications in order to continue looking after Janet – even though she had been part of their family for 20 years.

It is the perfect example of how rules and regulations get out of hand. A minister reads in the newspapers a terrible story – and a genuine one – about an old people's home which has been forced to close after it was trying to feed 20 OAPs on a fish pie made from one small tin of pilchards. They react by thinking: we must have some standards. A team of civil servants is sent away to dream up some ideas for a new bill – in the course of which, to use the favoured cant, they 'consult with all stakeholders'. The stakeholders, needless to say, are made up of vested interests who are able to twist the legislation to their advantage. The unions suggest regulations which create extra jobs. Large companies who are involved in the provision of the service in question suggest new regulations which make life easier for them – and considerably more difficult for their smaller competitors.

Before you know it the ministry has produced a hotch-potch of new rules each one of which pleases somebody or other but which add up to monstrous interference in an area of human activity which, disregarding the single instance which the minister read about, was actually working quite well. The end result, in the case of the Care Standards Act, was that people who had been nursing for 50 years are banned from care homes because they have not taken the latest vocational qualification, that dozens of perfectly good care homes have been forced to close and suddenly there is a dreadful shortage. In consequence, hospitals fill up with elderly 'bed-blockers' who cannot be discharged because there is nowhere else for them to go, operations are cancelled – and suddenly there is a huge scandal to replace the very minor scandal which kicked off the whole sorry business.

It is a tale repeated over and over again. Take some other fine examples of the Law of Unintended Consequences in action:

• Doctors' surgeries were encouraged to install video screens in their waiting rooms allowing patients to be fed adverts on a continuous loop. The purpose was to raise extra revenue – though it quickly emerged that the commercial interests most keen to advertise in the surgeries were 'claim-farming' law firms which encourage patients to sue their doctors for medical negligence.

• NICE, the National Institute for Clinical Excellence, was set up in 1999 with the responsibility for performing a cost/benefit analysis of new drugs. No new treatment may be administered by the NHS until it has been given the nod of approval by the quango's bureaucrats. That is fine in theory: after all, new drug treatments can be extremely expensive and the Government has a duty to the taxpayer to ensure that public money is spent wisely. However, there is little evidence that NICE has saved taxpayers a single penny: quite the opposite, it has merely introduced an extra layer of bureaucracy which prevents desperately ill patients receiving new treatments – while any money saved simply disappears into the running costs of NICE.

In spite of NICE's activities, Britain spends 182 euros per inhabitant per year treating cancer patients – more than any European country except Norway and Switzerland. Yet Britain's cancer survival rates are lower even than the official figures for Albania. One contributory factor to this record of non-achievement is that NICE is dragging its heels over the introduction of a bowel cancer drug called Capecitabine. NICE's bureaucrats have ruled that the drug, while more effective than an earlier drug, 5-FU, is too expensive. However, NICE's bizarre formula for working out whether or not a drug is value for money fails to take account of the cost of administering the drug. Although 5-FU is relatively cheap to buy, it needs to be administered intravenously in hospital: an extremely expensive process requiring stays in hospital. Capecitabine, by contrast, can be taken by the patient at home in the form of a pill – a process which would cost the NHS nothing.

Whether new drugs will continue to be developed, given the bureaucracy involved in testing them, is another matter. Since 1995, medical researchers carrying out medical trials have been subjected to 44 new sets of regulations. The Data Protection Act, designed to protect citizens from having

their privacy infringed through the wanton use of private information, has proved an especially difficult obstacle. Under the regulations, patients must now give their 'informed consent' to their medical records being used in any medical trial. That might sound reasonable, but it causes havoc in epidemiology – the branch of medical research which seeks to uncover the causes of diseases through the long-term study of patients' medical records. Among the achievements of epidemiology was the discovery, in the 1950s, that cigarette smoking causes lung cancer. In 2004, the man who made that discovery, Sir Richard Doll, declared that such a piece of research would now be extremely difficult to conduct. Many of the patients who had contracted lung cancer were dead by the time the study was conducted – and therefore not in the best position to give their informed consent to the research.

The Royal College of Psychiatrists wanted to conduct some research into the performance of mental health services for adolescents. The idea was to pick 300 patients and follow their progress through the health service. Within a few months the study had produced 5,929 pages of work.

And yet the study hadn't even begun – that was just the paperwork involved in gaining permission for the patients to be used in the study.

5

NOSING AROUND

OUR HOMES

"Whytehall holds 28,000 penne-pushers.
The Ministreys send 160,000 parchments,
120,000 before 1066"
Extract from The Domesday Book
(or at least my translation of the original Latin)

THE

legacy of the Domesday Book, of course, is to give encouragement to every government statistician, every council busybody in their obsessive campaign to collect data. Perhaps they imagine that 900 years hence fragments of their work, in turn, will be copied in facsimile and hung from the walls of every village pub.

Fragments, that is, of documents such as the new register of houses in multiple occupancy (HMOs) which local authorities must by law now compile. Landlords who let property to students have long had to obey fire regulations, building regulations and of course to declare their income to the taxman. But that, of course, was not enough. In April 2006 the Government decided that owners of HMOs must apply for a licence if they were to continue to let them. To do this they have to fill in a 32 page form for each property they own, giving the measurements of every room, and details of every washbasin, television and toaster which lie within them. Although the bureaucratic burden falls entirely upon the landlord, for some reason it is state officials who have decided they need to be compensated for their time. Some local authorities immediately announced that they would charge up to £1,000 for registering each property.

The effect of the legislation has been to put small landlords at a huge disadvantage compared with the large property companies which in recent years have been putting up large numbers of private student hostels in university towns. Needless to say, the legislation was introduced after much consultation with, er, the companies which run the hostels.

That, sadly, is all too typical of the way in which new regulations are visited upon us: with the warm approval of someone who is going to benefit from the pain suffered by the rest of us. It is an ill regulation, as it were, which blows no professional body or trade association any good.

Yet that is exactly what the Government has managed to create with its plans for Home Information Packs (HIPs): a set of regulations in which virtually nobody can see any benefit – even the professional bodies for whom it could have created extra work.

From 1 June 2007 it will be compulsory for anyone who wishes to place their home on the market to first compile a

HIP costing between £600 and £700 according to the Government (and up to £1,000 according to other professionals in the field). The HIP will include the title to the property, evidence of planning permission and copies of guarantees for any work done on the property and 'local searches' (which are supposed to reveal any nasty planning applications or decisions which could affect the property). More controversially, until the Government dropped this part of the scheme in July 2006, HIPs were going to have to include a 'home condition report'. This is a mini-survey which is supposed to offer buyers reassurance that the home they are buying is not suffering from any major defects. The reality is somewhat different. When I bought my last house the surveyor made a great fuss about supposed rising damp (which only showed up on his electronic meter) yet missed a rather more obvious source of damp: a hole in the roof.

The Government does not even pretend that a home condition report will uncover everything that might be wrong with a property – the 'home inspectors' who will be writing the reports are being trained only to investigate potential problems which are visible on the surface. They will not, for example, be lifting any floorboards. In the words of one Government adviser a Home Condition Report will be 'like a doctor examining a patient with his clothes on'.

At first, HIPs seemed a massive job-creation scheme for chartered surveyors. Remarkably, however, the surveyors' professional body, the Royal Institution of Chartered Surveyors (RICS), was very lukewarm, warning the Government repeatedly that there would not be enough Home Inspectors trained in time to make the scheme work. No happier were the associations representing estate agents and mortgage-lenders, who warned that the proposals could cause chaos in the housing market, as vendors dumped their homes on the market in order to beat the deadline before the new regulations came into force. Moreover, none of them could see how HIPs were possibly going to speed up the house-buying process: the very reason the Government wanted to introduce HIPs in the first place. The Council of Mortgage Lenders warned that in spite of a Home Condition Report banks and building societies would still have to send out surveyors to value properties on which they were advancing mortgages – meaning the buying process would take just as long as before.

Faced with the inevitable, the Government backed down. But not completely. In a typical fudge it insisted that while house-sellers would no longer have to pay for a Home Condition Report they would still have to pay for their home to have an energy rating – supposedly telling buyers how much they would have to pay to heat and light the home. This, it turns out, is obligatory under European legislation.

The cost of a HIP will still come to over £500 – less than originally estimated, but still a large burden on anyone selling a home. The Government's late change of heart, on the other hand, has caused huge inconvenience to people who had undertaken a change in career to train as Home Inspectors – at a cost of up to £10,000 each. But all is not lost: the Government kindly promised to set up a helpline in case any felt they needed counselling. How jolly kind.

Anyone who thinks they can escape the madness of 21st century bureaucracy by hiding inside their homes and locking the doors behind them is in for a nasty shock. These are just a few of the ways in which officialdom is catching up with homeowners:

• Residents who live in conservation areas now have to notify their local planning authority every time they want to carry out any works on a tree more than two metres in height. Trees, of course, are very important to the character of a neighbourhood, but they do have a mischievous habit of growing. The rule applies – theoretically at least – even if you want to remove half a dozen twigs.

• One Suffolk man wanted to convert his cellar into a granny flat for his elderly relatives. Fine, his local authority told him, but if you do so you will effectively be increasing the local housing stock by one unit, and therefore you must make a contribution towards local leisure facilities. So they sent him a bill for £802, to be put towards a new children's playground – not quite the ideal facility for his relatives, who were both in their 80s.

• If you sprayed pebbledash over your 18th century cottage you might – quite reasonably – expect a visit and a stiff fine from your local authority's heritage officers. So does that mean that if you buy an 18th century cottage which has been covered with pebbledash by a previous owner you are entitled to remove it and restore the building to its original appearance? Not in the wonderful world of heritage officers it doesn't. One unfortunate Cotswold homeowner did just that – only to be ordered to replace the pebbledash on the grounds that it was a very important and historic 1960s alteration.

• The owner of a Hampshire thatched cottage has had just as miserable an experience. Initially, he re-thatched his home in combed wheat reed, the material traditionally used for the job in his part of the country. Unfortunately, the constitution of straw has changed over the past half century. Wheat grown in Britain now contains elevated levels of nitrates from the fertilizers used – making the straw more prone to rot. After spending £27,000 thatching and re-thatching he gave up and, at a further cost of £20,000, replaced the roof with South African veldt grass instead – an equally natural product but more resistant to rot. Few observers would have been able to tell the difference – unless, that is, they were heritage officers employed by English Heritage. The organisation insisted that no, only local Hampshire straw could be used on a Hampshire cottage – and ordered him to strip off the roof and start again.

Needless to say, the Government applies a somewhat lower standard of aesthetic perfection to its own projects. While the dispute over the thatched roof rumbled on, the nearby Twyford Down, a local beauty spot adjoining the slopes of an ancient British fort, was bulldozed to make way for the six-lane M3. The Department of Transport resisted pressure for a half-mile tunnel which could have saved the chalk downland.

This is far from the only case of double standards in Government planning. Install an oil-fired central heating system and the building regulations demand that the oil tank be located a good distance from the property – very difficult to achieve in many gardens. Yet the explosive properties of fuel did not seem to worry the planners who allowed the Buncefield Oil Depot to be built just 150 yards from the nearest home, on the fringes of Hemel Hempstead in Hertfordshire. On 11 December 2005 the depot, which had a design capacity to store 34,000 tonnes of petrol and 15,000 tonnes of kerosene, exploded, damaging 300 homes and destroying 20 businesses. Six months on, still nobody was taking any responsibility.

To leave a house unattended for a week or two can be a risk: who knows whether you will return from holiday to find your home broken into, valuables stolen and the floor scattered with broken glass. For this reason, many homeowners have taken to using house-sitters. For the house-sitters, most of whom are retired people who enjoy a change of scenery, it is a case of sitting back and making themselves at home and watering the odd house plant. Few would consider it a full-time job. Except, that is, the Department for Work and Pensions, which has declared that house-sitters must be paid the national minimum wage of £5 an hour. Given that house-sitters work, theoretically 24 hours a day, this makes the business of looking after your house a pretty expensive business. But it doesn't end there. House-sitters must also be offered holiday pay (many of them actually consider themselves to be on holiday while they are house-sitting) and stakeholder pensions. Moreover, before a house-sitter can begin work, a full scale 'risk assessment' must be carried out on the house.

One wall of a fire station in Gateshead had to be rebuilt at a cost of £25,000 after planners decreed that the bricks were the wrong shade of red – they were slightly too orange. When the rebuilding was complete nearby residents remarked that they couldn't tell the difference – "it looks just like the old wall". And yet, while absurdly pedantic in some respects, planning rules often allow developers to take outrageous liberties. In 1989 a developer won planning permission to build a block of apartments on the beach at Carlyon Bay, Cornwall. The development was not built and the planning permission, which only lasts five years, should have lapsed. In 2003, however, a second developer managed to persuade the local authority, Restormel, that it had made a start on the project and therefore should be allowed to finish it. And what 'start' had it made? It had painted a few white lines in the car park.

The problem is that the original plans approved in 1989 incorporate a sea wall which no longer meets modern standards, and therefore it cannot be built. While the developers battle it out with planners and protesters, one of the finest beaches in Cornwall is reduced to a building site – a wonderful advert for the planning system.

The Government in 2004 challenged housebuilders to cut the cost of new homes by devising more efficient methods of construction, which would allow new homes to be built for £60,000 each. It would be an easier task if a flurry of building regulations introduced over the past few years had not added between £4,500 and £7,000 to the cost of building an average flat. Among the new rules is an obligation to perform tests to check that new homes are sufficiently airtight – in order to cut draughts, save fuel and cut greenhouse emissions. It is only possible to pass these tests if the windows are built with strips of draught excluder. However, somebody pointed out that if houses were all built this way their occupants would run out of oxygen – hence the regulations now also compel windows to have air vents, thus making a nonsense of the requirement for draught excluders.

It is now illegal to replace a window without installing double-glazing. This puts owners of listed buildings in an impossible position, because many of them have been told by conservation officers that it is illegal to install double-glazing.

Moreover, homeowners who fit new windows have, since 2002, been obliged to get approval from their local authority building control department – at a typical cost of £60. This cost covers a visit from the local building control officer to make sure your new windows conform to fire and insulation standards – and use toughened, rather than ordinary, glass. Large window-replacement companies, on the other hand, are allowed to 'certify' the quality of their own work – providing they belong to FENSA, the industry's self-certification scheme. Members qualify for this not by taking any qualifications but simply by being able to show they have been in business for two years, having insurance and having access to the internet or a fax machine. Not all appear to be able to meet the required standards. In an attempt to assure the quality of the scheme, members of FENSA have one per cent of their installations inspected by an outside firm. In 2003, after the scheme had been running a year, the Office of the Deputy Prime Minister (ODPM) reported that FENSA members had failed 16.5 per cent of their inspections – most often because they had failed to obey the fire regulations.

Homeowners are also now expected to seek building regulation approval for a variety of other works, including alterations to drains and installation of new electrical circuits. The regulations have become a nonsense: most local authorities interviewed by the ODPM in 2003 admitted that hardly any homeowners bothered to seek approval when undertaking these installations – and that the local authorities hadn't a clue when such works were being undertaken.

However...

The conservation laws do not seem to apply to everyone – most notably the Government itself when it wants to build new airports. In 2004 the Department for Culture, Media and Sport introduced new, 'tougher' heritage legislation, hidden deep inside which was one innocuous-sounding sentence: in future the decision whether or not to list a property should be undertaken "in the context of the future of the area in which the building stands". It put this policy into practice by refusing to give a Grade I listing to St Mary's church in Harmondsworth, Middlesex, a remarkable building which boasts a 14th century chancel and a 12th century south arcade. The reason? Ministers quite fancy the site for Heathrow's third runway. Instead of being listed, the culture secretary suggested instead that it be recorded – i.e. that it should be photographed before being demolished. While that might prove handy for future scholars, it doesn't exactly promote the public's enjoyment of a 14th century church.

Some rules and regulations are so bizarre that no matter how many times you look at them, they still don't make any sense, and you are left scratching your head, thinking: who the hell comes up with this stuff? This is one of them:

In the spring of 2006 several water companies in the south-east of England imposed hosepipe bans in order to save water, after a dryish year in which this part of the country saw only 78 per cent normal rainfall. The ban prevented homeowners from watering the plants in their garden or cleaning their car with the aid of a hose. However, here are a few things which the hosepipe ban, imposed under the powers of the Water Act 1991, somehow omitted to prohibit:

Filling your swimming pool with a hose
Hosing down your driveway or garden path
(so long as you do not water the flowerbeds
in the process)
Cleaning a motorcycle with a hose
Going to a garage and cleaning your car with
a high-pressure hose
Having a water fight using a hose

And needless to say, the water restrictions don't seem to apply to our leaders at all. Soon after a hosepipe ban was introduced in Surrey, passers-by noticed that a sprinkler system was being used to water flowers along the driveway leading to a house owned by Geoffrey Robinson, Labour MP and former Government minister. Outraged, they rang the water company to complain – only to be told that what Mr Robinson was doing was entirely within the law. His property was served by a private borehole through which he is allowed to extract 22,000 gallons every day – no matter that the water was coming from the same underground aquifers as the public water supply.

And if it is any consolation…

Homeowners who feel aggrieved by excessive regulation over their premises might just feel a pang of sympathy for the banks (not always the most popular institutions). Banks who set up stand-alone cashpoint machines in garages and shopping centres have found themselves sent bills for water rates – even though the machines are fully automated, don't drink coffee and don't ever need a pee.

6

DIVERSITY

Domestic Violence Co-ordinator
Public sector job description

I F you were wheeled into a hospital accident and emergency department you might expect the first questions to be along the lines of 'how do you feel?' and 'where does it hurt?' Those questions, however, can wait. There is one question which NHS staff must, as a priority, now ask all their patients: "to which ethnic group do you belong?"

Britons, like worms in a biological laboratory, are now officially divided into 15 species and 65 sub-species according to their ethnicity. You might be 'White British' (WBRI) or a Traveller of Irish Heritage (WIRT), a Black Carribean (BCRB) or – presumably a category designed especially for the zebra community – a 'White and Black African' (MWBA).

The data must by law be collected by all public bodies so that it can be analysed by the country's 'diversity officers'. It is all in the name, apparently, of ironing out racial inequality once and for all. Except that it seems to be achieving exactly the opposite. The sole black applicant for a job as a dustman

in Manchester was eliminated – on the grounds
that when filling out his application form he
had overlooked the section on 'ethnic
awareness'.

The organiser of a
Northamptonshire harp festival
was refused a grant because he
had failed to demonstrate, on his
'cultural diversity monitoring form'
that his event was sufficiently multi-
ethnic. In fact, he had flown over a
team of Paraguayan harpists for the
event – but he couldn't enter them on his
form because South Americans, according to the official
classification scheme, do not exist.

The nation's diversity officers have, needless to say, used
data to eradicate some appalling injustices of modern Britain.
Among them are:

1. The Lake District National Park announced that it was
   to stop free guided tours on the basis that not enough
   hikers from the ethnic minorities were taking them up.

2. A Bristol pub landlord was served with an Anti-Social Behaviour Order (which carries the threat of five years imprisonment if broken) for displaying a sign saying 'The Porking Yard' – on the grounds that it could be offensive to muslims who pray at a mosque in the street. In fact, the sign was derived from the fact that the street used to be known as Pork Alley as it contained several butchers' shops.

3. Angie Sayer, the landlady of the New Inn at Wedmore in Somerset, was visited by Police investigating a complaint of 'incitement to racial hatred' – because she had flown a Welsh flag during a St George's Day archery competition.

4. The DVLA has withdrawn the car registration plate GO05TEP on the grounds that it might be offensive to Germans.

5. The diversity officers of one primary care trust sprung into action after discovering that 'not enough Pakistani and Bangladeshi women were using the trust's sexual health services'. One might have thought it a complement to the strong belief in marriage among

Pakistani and Bangladeshi communities that few women needed to seek treatment for venereal diseases, but not in the wonderful world of diversity: the primary care trust immediately scattered the district with sexually-explicit leaflets imploring women to seek treatment for diseases they almost certainly hadn't got.

Schools have been ordered not only to produce an annual ethnic monitoring survey, but also to formulate a policy promoting racial equality. The first draft, demands the Commission for Racial Equality, should be drawn up by the headteacher, several other teachers, governors and representatives from the pupils' council. Then it must be sent to unions and local community groups for comment, before being promoted via a poster campaign 'in all the main languages used in the community' before finally being adopted. All in all, the task amounts to several weeks' work – all in the cause of stating the blindingly obvious: this school does not discriminate on the grounds of race.

At least one piece of commonsense has been written into the instructions sent to public servants informing them of their duties to collect ethnic data. A 34 page document distributed to NHS staff helpfully suggests how procedures can be varied in the case of one class of patient. "The temporarily confused or traumatised (including the unconscious): there will be instances when it is more appropriate to collect some data later in the admission."

In common with an increasing number of laws, the Employment Equality Regulations 2003 were never debated in Parliament, being introduced instead as a 'statutory instrument'. Yet they impose huge new costs on businesses. For example, companies are forbidden, under threat of huge compensation claims, from advertising, say, for a husband and wife team to run a sports club: the advert is deemed to discriminate against gay couples. Employers have also been warned that they must take into account the religious needs of all their staff. Here is a selection of things which employers have been warned not to do:

1. Hold important meetings on 31 October – it might discriminate against pagans, who, of course, celebrate the festival of Samhain on that day.

2. Hold a Christmas party in a hotel – it might make muslim members of staff feel left out. A muslim insurance salesman from Bristol took his employers to a tribunal because they were in the habit of offering bottles of wine as rewards to employees who met their sales

targets. He complained that he felt left out because he was not allowed to drink the prize.

3. Suggest that a Jain should work at sunset, when he needs to pray. (But what if he is a lollipop man, and the children need to get home before dark?)

Besides the requirement to demonstrate that they have not discriminated on religious grounds, employers are also warned that they must not discriminate on the grounds of gender or sexual orientation. Companies are warned they may be fined if they:

• Advertise a job 'which would be suitable for a married couple' – the advert would discriminate against single people. Yet there are jobs, such as caretaker of a hostel, which require two people and furthermore require them to live on site in single premises. To employ two single people for such a job would require huge extra expense.

• Ask, in a job interview, an innocent question about an applicant's family – it might be seen as discriminatory against gay couples.

• Hold office parties in lap-dancing clubs, which might make gay employees feel uncomfortable.

Employment tribunals have become a huge drain on British business, with seemingly little redress for a business accused of discrimination: being taken to a tribunal can cost thousands of pounds in legal costs, yet a company cannot claim costs against a claimant, even if the case he brings is clearly without foundation. One claimant, a Nigerian surveyor by training, managed to bring 72 private companies and public sector bodies to employment tribunals through their failure to offer him a job. The would-be employers incurred £500,000 in legal costs – in spite of evidence that the surveyor was not qualified to undertake the jobs for which he had applied.

In 2003 the Government, again using a 'statutory

instrument' in order to avoid Parliamentary debate, reversed the onus of proof in discrimination cases. Now, the employee bringing the action does not have to prove he is the victim of discrimination; the employer defending it has to prove that he has not acted in a discriminatory way.

Assuming, that is, the employer was not faced with circumstances which actually require him to act in a discriminatory fashion. The perversity of the Government's diversity agenda is that in some cases the rules can be turned on their head − if by doing so the diversity industry can achieve the 'right' result. Twenty-three year old Kieran Keenan thought he had found the ideal job as a trainee museum assistant at the Royal Pavilion in Brighton. Until, that is, he was told he could not apply on the basis that he wasn't African, Afro-Caribbean, Asian or Chinese. These ethnic groups, said Brighton and Hove council, only make up 3.6 per cent of its workforce − a little lower than the 4.5 per cent target which it had set itself.

So what is an employer supposed to do: ignore a job applicant's colour and give the job to the best-qualified candidate − or count up the number of members of ethnic groups on his staff and deliberately pick out a candidate whose face matches any under-represented group? The employer is in an impossible position, damned if he does, damned if he doesn't. The only sure thing is that there will always be plenty of work for bureaucrats in the race relations industry – who, like Basil Fawlty telling his staff 'don't mention the war' to a group of German guests – have become so obsessed with stamping out racial discrimination that they end up committing the very offence they set out to avoid.

Here is but one example: a female applicant for a job in the police was rejected after she was asked, in an interview, whom she would contact if she needed help. She suggested that she would talk to her sergeant – the correct answer, except that she referred to the sergeant as 'him' – an act which betrayed her latent sexist attitudes and, in the eyes of the police, made her unworthy of the job.

By the way…

…any non-Indians who think that ethnic quotas will make them a shoe-in for a job in an Indian restaurant can forget it: the Race Relations Act decrees that in such cases employers are allowed to discriminate in order to create an authentic dining experience.

And then of course, there is disability legislation:

The Government makes great play of the fact that it consults over every new piece of legislation. Goodness knows how many trees have been felled in the production of the now ubiquitous 'consultation document' which invariably runs to several dozen, if not hundreds of pages. Just a little example of what this hugely expensive process achieves:

Unless their owners can prove that it would be impractical to do so, all commercial premises must, under the provisions of the Disability Discrimination Act, now be made fully accessibly to disabled people. Businesses who fail to meet the new rules face stiff fines. The Government proudly declared that it had asked 200 consultees before introducing the legislation. Yet only two of these – the British Chambers of Commerce and the Licensed Victuallers Association, represented the owners of business premises. Others were pressure groups, quangos, or trade bodies such as the Contract Flooring Association, which has a vested interest in businesses being forced to make physical changes to their buildings.

Among those affected were the nuns at Tyburn Convent in London. For years they have happily been showing visitors around their crypt, which boasts the remains of Reformation martyrs. However, the crypt is accessible only via winding steps, and inaccessible to the disabled. In order to comply with the Disability Discrimination Act the nuns were told that they must spend £400,000 installing ramps and a lift – an impossible sum to raise considering the convent has only 25 nuns.

A couple more absurdities from the world of anti-disability discrimination:

• South West Trains, which runs services out of London's Waterloo station, was ordered to remove 28 trains from its fleet because the lettering on the electronic strips inside the carriages which tell you the next station were only 32 mm high – rather than the approved 35 mm. The trains had to be removed after a complaint from the Disabled Persons Transport Advisory Committee, which argued that partially-sighted passengers might have trouble reading the information.

The fact that the trains had been built before the new regulations came into force seemed to count for nothing. Neither did the fact that passengers were simultaneously read out the next station over the tannoy system.

The result of the withdrawal of the trains was that South West Trains ended up with a shortage of rolling stock. Trains which had previously been formed of eight carriages were suddenly formed of only four. The outcome was overcrowding and more people standing – hardly in the interests of disabled passengers.

• The owner of a Suffolk caravan park was ordered to pay £2,000 in compensation to a couple who complained after he turned down their booking for April, suggesting that it would be better if they came in June, when the ground would be drier and they were less likely to get their wheelchairs stuck in the mud. He was also ordered to go on a 'disability awareness' course – in spite of the fact that he, himself, is disabled. The result? Peeved businessman closes down caravan park. The able-bodied jump on aeroplanes and holiday cheaply in countries where there is little or no health and safety legislation. As for the disabled, who find aeroplane travel difficult, they have lost yet another facility.

7

BELT AND BRACES
AND ELASTIC
AND VELCRO TOO

In the event of fire,
close all doors and windows before leaving room
Sign on back of hotel room door, Grenoble, France

"WE want to save lives, not tie businesses up in red tape. Good risk assessment is the way to achieve this." So said Jonathan Rees, the chief executive of the Government's safety quango, the Health and Safety Executive (HSE), while launching his latest publication, Five Steps to Risk Assessment, in 2006. Needless to say, while saying one thing his quango was doing the other. The document described the procedure which companies must now go through in order to ensure that their premises meet health and safety regulations. The document includes a three page sample 'risk assessment' carried out by an enlightened office manager, who, for example, sniffed around the office for risky electrical appliances and 'instructed staff not to bring their own kettles into work as maintenance cannot be assured'. Instead, he took out a contract with a coffee machine manufacturer.

All that this swot achieved, of course, was to prevent staff from enjoying a cuppa of freshly-brewed tea and coffee in proper cups and instead made them drink an expensive concoction of powdered matter tasting of pee from plastic cups, which are much more likely to cause spillage and burns. Nevertheless, the quest for perfect safety goes on. Among the other recent initiatives of the HSE is a 'ladder amnesty' for Yorkshire tradesmen to dispose of ladders with missing rungs and the publication of the 'Managing Workforce Transport Risk and Routemap', a 29 page document which suggests ways in which companies should seek to reduce accidents involving vehicles. Among the wisdoms are:

"It should be possible to prevent vehicles from moving, for example, by applying the brakes and removing the keys."

Hauliers, bus companies and taxi firms who had never previously thought of fixing brakes to their vehicles have no doubt picked up some useful tips.

The HSE went one better with a leaflet entitled Dry-Cleaners: Are you in control?, appealing to the owners of dry-cleaning shops to guard against disaster. It began:

Most people don't consider dry-cleaning to be a dangerous industry. But just consider the following:

• A dry-cleaner is electrocuted because of faulty electrics.

- An employee is found unconscious having tried to mop up a spill of cleaning solvent.
- Customers are hurt when a perchloroethylene machine explodes during distillation.
- An outbreak of legionnaires' disease is traced to a dry-cleaner's wet cooling tower.
- Major structural damage is caused when a steam boiler blows up.

All nightmare scenarios for the dry cleaning industry and costly in many different ways. But none of them need happen if the dry-cleaner is in control of health and safety

Curious, I rang up the HSE to ask them how many recorded instances there were of the above disasters. Er, they couldn't think of any, though they did suggest that some dry-cleaners had injured their backs stooping down to pick up baskets.

Where to start with the great achievements of the health and safety police? Here are a few tasters:

• Bristol City Council spent £5,000 planting a hundred yew trees at the Blaise Castle Estate. Several months later they were dug up after a 'risk assessment' determined that they could be dangerous to children. Safety experts claimed that children could fall ill with diarrhoea if they ate 'several handfuls' of the foliage.

• Not to be outdone, Norwich City Council ordered 20 horse chestnut trees to be cut down on the grounds that passers-by might be injured if children threw sticks to bring down conkers.

• Taking its duty to protect the public even more seriously, Cheltenham Borough Council banned the planting of pansies in town centre flowerbeds. It was worried that its gardeners might hurt their wrists if they caught their trowels on tree roots.

• Neighbouring Tewkesbury Council went one better: it banned paper napkins being presented to meals-on-wheels customers – for fear that their recipients might mistake them for an item of food and choke on them.

• You can't be too careful where food is involved. In an effort to persuade children to eat more fruit and vegetables, the Government spent £42 million on a National Fruit Scheme. Children at 2,500 schools were regularly sent free fruit. And, just to be on the safe side, each box included detailed instructions – on how to eat a carrot. (You are supposed to start by nibbling it from the bottom, by the way.)

• Firemen in Greater Manchester were sent four pages of

instructions and given specialist training on how to sit down on their new reclining chairs – even though the chairs required only one pull of a lever to be lowered into reclining position. A spokesman for the Fire Service said specialist training was required because 'there are moving parts'. A Southampton fire station, meanwhile, has been built without a pole because chiefs decided that firemen might sprain their ankles while descending to their engines in an emergency. Instead, the firemen will have to run down three flights of stairs – a far more hazardous thing to do than sliding down a pole.

It is not always practical or possible, of course, to offer training on the safe way to undertake such complex and hazardous tasks as eating a carrot or sitting in a chair. In such cases, sadly, the only option is to ban the dangerous activity. Here are just a few examples of things which have been rendered illegal in Britain in recent years:

• Cardiff bus passenger Brian Heale was refused passage on a bus – on the grounds that he was carrying a tin of emulsion paint.

• Contractors in Kirkby Lonsdale, Cumbria, were forbidden from climbing ladders to change lightbulbs on street lamps. The council is now considering spending £1,000 a time on folding lamp-posts which eradicate the need for ladders.

• War veterans in Walton-on-the-Naze, Essex were banned from firing gun salutes to mark the beginning and end of the two minutes silence on Remembrance Sunday. It was feared that debris might blow back inland – in spite of the fact that the practice has been going on for 60 years without record of a single injury.

• Pubs in Kent, which have for many years been decorating their bars with bundles of dry hops, have been ordered by health and safety officers to remove them – or replace them with plastic hops.

• Restaurants are now banned from allowing a single fiddler to serenade guests – unless they apply for a full entertainment licence.

• The landlord of the Melbourne pub in York was forced to warn his customers to remain in their seats whenever a pub singer was performing. He was threatened with a fine of up to £20,000 when an elderly drinker got up and performed an impromptu gig.

It gets worse...

Elaine Richards baked a birthday cake for a 96 year old friend living in a nursing home in Barnstaple. Shortly before the party was due to start, Mrs Richards received a call from the nursing home telling her regretfully that consumption of the cake would not be allowed on the premises because of hygiene regulations. The rules insisted that only cakes bought in shops could be eaten by residents.

It seems this advice derives directly from the Food Standards Agency, the Government's food quango. Its public information website, eatwell, contains the following advice: "Foods such as home-made mayonnaise, ice cream, cake mix and mousses can contain raw eggs and therefore carry a risk of salmonella... Commercial products are made using pasteurized egg, which is egg that has been heated to kill bacteria, including salmonella. Commercial products may also contain an acidifying agent which will kill bacteria."

The message, then, is simple: eat home-made food and you will get ill. Stick to safe, shop-bought goods, on the other hand, and you will be just fine. Just the one problem: if shop-bought products are so disease-free why did Cadburys plc have to recall several million bars of chocolate in June 2006 after finding them to be infected with a rare strain of salmonella? Okay, it was an accident and I am sure the problem has been sorted. But it does beg the question: is there some friend of the processed food industry out there who is advising the Government on healthy-eating advice?

Not that food-processing companies are immune from petty rules and regulations. A Merseyside drinks company received a letter from the Advertising Standards Authority warning it that the actors used in an advert for an alcoholic drink were too attractive. "We would advise that the men in the picture should be unattractive – i.e. overweight, middle-aged, balding etc. In its current form we consider that the advert is in danger of implying that the drink may bring sexual/social success."

A few more things which have been banned on safety grounds:

• The villagers of Ardmore in the Scottish Highlands have lost their postal service because the Royal Mail decided that the one and a half mile long path to their village was too dangerous to be negotiated by a postman. The path is classified by the local tourist board as 'an easy walk'.

• Manufacturers of church organs were horrified to learn that lead organ pipes could be banished under the EU

Restriction of Hazardous Substances Directive. After some thought the European Commission's Technical Advisory Committee decided that, given that people do not tend to drink water through organ pipes, they could be exempted from the rules.

• Soldiers learning the bagpipes have been banned from playing for more than 24 minutes a day. The Army Medical Directorate arrived at the figure after a study which concluded that the pipes could reach 111 decibels. Too bad, presumably, if the army band happens to be playing a piece of music 25 minutes long.

• Residents in a council block in Bow, East London, were ordered to remove their window boxes – on the grounds that they were a danger to the public. The council's insurers argued that the boxes could fall on people's heads. There isn't a great deal of evidence for their fear: in fact the Royal Society for the Prevention of Accidents recorded just two injuries involving window boxes in 2004 – and they involved people standing on the boxes and falling off. What window boxes do achieve, of course, is to brighten up an otherwise grim inner city area. Muggings in the local area run at hundreds per year.

• The resort of Torquay, Devon, prospered in the 19th century on its reputation as the 'English Riviera', a title earned by the presence of palm trees which thrive in its mild, maritime climate. In 2006, however, council officials declared palm trees to be a terrible danger to the public, complaining that the tree can "cause injury to eyes/faces if inappropriately placed". A few weeks earlier the council, a unitary authority, had also closed the town's promenade, on the grounds that it was crumbling and could cause a danger to the public. Presumably, the next project will be to drain the sea in order to prevent the possibility of anybody drowning.

The Government wants children to take more exercise, to prevent them turning into obese adults. But how, given that it is in some cases illegal for them to exercise? Many municipal swimming pools now impose a rule which says that all children under five must have one-to-one supervision from an adult at all times. This makes it impossible for many families ever to visit a pool: if you have a child aged four and two twins aged two, for example, it is impossible for you to go swimming unless you borrow an extra adult. I asked one local authority why it had imposed such a rule at its swimming pools, and was told that it had been advised to do

so in a series of manuals which it had bought from a body called the Institute of Sports and Recreational Management, which seems to do very well out of advising people not to do things. Among its publications are the Risk Assessment Manual (£245 plus VAT), Effective Pool Supervision video (£180) and the Health and Safety Management two video pack (£244).

The parish council in Great Somerford, Wiltshire, was forced to spend £2,500 to replace children's swings. The old swings had been condemned because the top of the frame stood 22 inches above the maximum height specified in an EU directive on playground safety. (Since this rule was enforced, interestingly, even the Royal Society for the Prevention of Accidents has expressed its concern that playgrounds are becoming too 'boring'. Spokesman David Yearley warned that children brought up in surroundings which are too safe will simply seek thrills elsewhere: such as on railway lines.)

And worse....

A popular line of jokes in the 1980s concerned the changing of lightbulbs. As in: *how many social workers does it take to change a lightbulb? None, but it takes 17 to organise a seminar on 'coping with darkness'.* How we laughed. Or at least we laughed until the EU Working at Heights Directive came along. Then it ceased to be a joke.

The priest at a catholic church in Beccles, Suffolk, used to change his lightbulbs by sending one man up a ladder. The cost was minimal. Under the new directive, however, the practice was banned. Instead, he was told that he must hire scaffolding. To change a couple of lightbulbs took two days and cost him £1,300. That was modest, though, compared with the bill run up by the BBC for installing nine shelves – it came to £2,500.

It is a good job that the Working at Heights Directive does not apply to God himself: presumably his services would have to cease until he could find safer accommodation than a perch in the clouds. The regulations are deemed to apply, however, to acrobats employed by the Moscow State Circus: they were warned that for any performance which took place at a height above that of the average stepladder (just try performing an acrobatics routine at a height lower than this) acrobats must wear hard hats.

The events of 11 September 2001 have left a huge, indelible mark on global politics. They have also managed to usher in a whole new era of regulation. Whereas before the Government may have had trouble explaining why it wanted – say – to outlaw hat-pins, now it merely has to utter one magic word – 'terror' – and suddenly every bizarre rule and regulation can be justified. Of course it may inconvenience the public if they are no longer allowed to use hat pins/leave rubbish in rubbish bins/go on holiday with a nail file/[fill in just about any everyday object or activity you like], but with the terrorist threat you can never be too careful.

Needless to say, when terrorist acts really do occur – as they did in London on 7 July 2005 – the legislation passed in the name of terrorism invariably turns out to be irrelevant. Take the issue of Identity Cards, which Britons will soon have to buy themselves – at an estimated cost of £80 each. The Home Office has repeatedly justified the cards on the basis of countering the terrorist threat. Pointedly, however, the four suicide bombers who struck on the Underground – while the bill was still being debated in Parliament – made no attempt to conceal their identity whatsoever. The security services knew exactly who they were, and that their ring-leader had connections with terrorist groups, but gave up monitoring him. One can't necessarily criticise them for this: there were many individuals believed to pose a higher threat, and the Police only have so many eyes and ears. But it does show the utter pointlessness of ID cards, and suggest that huge amounts of time could be wasted checking people with irregularities in their ID cards – while the real terrorists, not seeking to hide their identity, only their intentions, escape detection.

A few more bizarre rules and regulations which have been justified in the name of terror:

• Under the Serious Organised Crime and Police Act of 2005 it is now against the law to carry out any political demonstration within a kilometre of Parliament Square without first seeking permission from the Commissioner of the Metropolitan Police.

• In the six months following the World Trade Center attacks of 11 September 2001, airport security staff confiscated thousands of nail files and tweezers from passengers' luggage – on the grounds that they might possibly be used as weapons by hijackers. Yet at the same time duty-free shops were allowed to continue selling booze in glass bottles which, if broken by a terrorist could be turned into far deadlier weapons. Security was paramount, in other words, until it was deemed to interfere with the duty-free industry.

• The European Union gave in to demands from the US to hand over the 'Passenger Name Records' of every airline passenger who has checked in to a transatlantic flight. The data includes such vital aids in the fight against terrorism as passengers' credit card details and what they ordered for their in-flight meal. American Airlines, incidentally, stopped the practice of handing over this data on internal flights after outraged passengers complained at the invasion of their privacy.

• Following the discovery of a plot to blow up transatlantic airliners in August 2006, there was heightened security at all buildings around London. The Conservative politician, Iain Dale, was not the least surprised, then, to be asked, while entering the ITN building one evening, to present his briefcase for inspection. He was alarmed, however, when the security guard, having opened the suitcase, then refused to sift through it for weapons or explosives. He wasn't allowed to, the guard explained: it was all because of health and safety rules. I mean, he added, "there could be anything in there". Of course there could: you don't want to risk one of your security guards cutting himself on a terrorist's machete, do you?

• And don't forget 82 year old Walter Wolfgang, a lifelong Labour party member who was frogmarched from the 2005 Labour party conference and held under the Terrorism Act for shouting out 'that's a lie and you know it' to the foreign secretary during a debate on the Iraq war.

It is reassuring to know that the Government is protecting us, if not against suicide-bombers, then against elderly men with a habit of not putting up their hands before they speak.

8

THE

EUROPEAN UNION

EUROPE, in popular imagination, is the land of straight bananas where carrots are designated as fruits and where a spade is called a hand-propelled earth-extraction device. Not everything said and written about the European Union is true, including the sometime rumour that the EU is to ban mushy peas. However, it says something about the organisation's fervour for bureaucracy that it feels the need to classify every 'euromyth' which it spots in the press.

First the good news. The European Union appears to have realised that it is held in contempt for its bureaucratic obsessions. In September 2005, the head of the European Commission, José Manuel Barroso, announced that he was to launch a crackdown on red tape. No fewer than 69 legislative proposals, he said, would be reviewed and many might be scrapped. Among them was the proposed Optical Radiation Directive (sunlight to you and me) which would have obliged employers to make sure that their employees always covered up to protect themselves from sun burn. The proposal had become unpopular among German barmaids, who have a long-held tradition of wearing skimpy tops while on duty, and even more so with their customers.

Now the bad news. Even if every one of these 69 directives does get cancelled, that will still leave 22,000 EU regulations running to a total of 83,000 pages. Moreover, the regulatory burden of EU regulations is growing exponentially. According to the think tank Open Europe, in the first 40 years of the EU's existence, between 1957 and 1997, there were 10,000 regulations. In the seven years thereafter there were 12,000.

Regulations, that is, like the Directive on Rail Safety, designed to enforce safety on high speed lines – but also applicable to heritage steam lines where the trains run at a maximum of 25 mph. Several of the railways, which are run

by volunteers and do not make profits, were threatened with closure after being told that they must hire rail inspectors at a cost of £200 an hour.

…and regulations such as the EU Directive on Vibration and Noise at Work which was introduced with lorries and buses in mind but now threatens to paralyse the British Army after military engineers pointed out that it is impossible to meet the required standards on vibration when firing a round from a Challenger tank. The Army now faces having to order its troops to have a rest midway through a tank offensive because they have exceeded the number of hours which they are allowed to spend in a vibration environment.

…not forgetting the Working Time Directive which Britain thought it had opted out of during negotiations for the Maastricht Treaty in the early 1990s but which the European Commission managed to introduce through the back door as a 'health and safety' measure. It is now the single biggest burden on British business. Obliging Britons to work no more than a 48 hour week, it is estimated by the Government's own Regulatory Impact Assessments to have cost British industry the grand sum of £13.6 billion since it was introduced in 1999.

In case you are wondering, the next four biggest EU-inspired burdens are:

1. Vehicle Excise Duty (Reduced Pollution) (Amendment) Regulations: cumulative cost £5.513 billion.

2. Data Protection Act: £5.347 billion.

3. Control of Asbestos at Work: £1.393 billion.

4. Not forgetting the awkwardly-named Disability Discrimination (Providers of Services) (Adjustments from 1999 of Premises) Regulations 2004: £1.208 billion.

What did the European Commission do to mitigate the impact of these regulations on business before they were introduced? Virtually nothing. According to the British Chambers of Commerce a mere 1 in 200 EU regulations are actually subjected to an impact assessment before they are introduced. And even then the EU might as well not have bothered: the EU's impact-assessment criteria has not found a single EU regulation to have a negative impact.

So that's alright, then. Or rather it isn't. It is quite clear that whatever noises the EU may make from time to time about cutting bureaucracy, it does not mean a word of it. If it did, it would long since have dropped its commitment to the EU constitution. This 333 page document, designed to establish the EU for the first time as a legal polity is the most bizarre constitution ever written: binding, for example, EU countries to a policy on space exploration. It is one thing for the EU to have a policy on space exploration now, but will that same policy still be relevant in, say, 500 years' time when many of us are living on Mars and shopping on Jupiter? It is as if the US constitution had committed the country forever after to a policy on horses and carts – which might have seemed sensible in 1776, but is rather less relevant now.

The constitution has been ratified by several European countries. But, crucially, where the matter has been put to a referendum, it has been rejected. In May 2005 French voters rejected it by 55 per cent to 45 per cent. A few days later voters in the Netherlands rejected it by 62 per cent to 38 per cent. Clearly, according to the rules, the treaty should have been dead.

But that is not how the EU works. The EU's approach to referenda can be summed up in that old schoolboy's motto: 'if at once you don't succeed, try, try, try again.' That is what happened with Maastricht, with the Nice Treaty and may well yet happen with the EU Constitution. Already, the EU has been caught trying to introduce measures contained within the treaty through the back door.

It isn't always easy to determine exactly which bizarre

rules and regulations derive from Brussels and which have been home-grown in Whitehall. The EU makes its legislation in the form of directives which it is then up to national governments to incorporate into domestic law, some leeway being allowed in how the directive is interpreted. When faced with examples of foolish laws, keen supporters of the EU tend to accuse the Government of 'gold-plating' European directives as they are incorporated into domestic law. Is this fair? The think tank Open Europe thinks not. It has analysed the 3,000 new regulations which come into force every year and concluded that 77 per cent of the cost of meeting new regulations derives from Brussels, the remainder being put down to home-grown regulations or the 'gold-plating' of EU directives.

While we are on the subject, here is a directive which has clearly been 'gold-plated':

• Barley straw has been used for several centuries for killing off algae in ponds. But in 2003 the Health and Safety Executive decided that under the European Biocidal Products Directive barley straw must be treated as if it were a brand new pesticide introduced onto the market. It could not be sold for controlling algae unless it first underwent two years of trials – costing nearly £200,000. Clearly, the directive itself is rational: pesticides which get into the food chain can cause huge environmental damage. It is the interpretation of the directive to include a natural product which has been used safely for thousands of years which is the nonsense – a 'gold-plated' directive if there ever was one.

But then again, here are a few pieces of nonsense straight from Brussels:

• The EU has managed the remarkable topographical feat of removing thousands of islands from the map. According to EU bureaucracy an island is no longer an island if:

It has fewer than 50 permanent inhabitants
It lies less than one kilometre from the main-land
It houses the capital of an EU state

The EU justified the move on the grounds that its islands budget was running out of control. Yet rather than trying to change the map, why didn't it just change the system whereby it automatically doles out grants to people who live on islands?

• Regulation (EC) 1/2005 on the protection of animals during transportation demands that all lorries carrying farm animals long distances must be equipped with satellite navigation equipment. Excellent news for manufacturers of satellite navigation systems, but what's in it for the animals? Not a lot, if the experience of motorists is anything to go by. Residents of the North Yorkshire hamlet of Crackpot were puzzled as to why dozens of vehicles were getting stuck up an unmade track, with a sheer 100 foot drop on one side, until one of the lost motorists told them that he had taken the advice of his new satnav system. The same happened to Wiltshire residents who found themselves repeatedly hauling lost motorists out of a four foot deep ford. At least it is going to make travelling more fun for cows and sheep, but I'm not so sure about protecting them.

• The EU Hazardous Waste Directive has a noble enough aim: to reduce the quantities of harmful chemicals being disposed of in the environment. But does it really need to be so dogmatic? Intercare, a Leicester-based charity, has for 30 years been collecting surplus medicines from the National Health Service and sending them to seven African nations where medicines are otherwise hard to come by. That was until the Environment Agency decided that medicines are hazardous waste – and henceforth must be buried in hazardous waste sites in Britain.

• An Irish company which applied to register a domain

name with the ending .eu was charged 254 euros, then asked to provide a company certificate of registration. This was not enough: it was then asked to swear an affidavit that it had a genuine claim to the domain name.

• Trainspotters might be regarded by many people as sad, but a danger to the public? They have been banished from many stations in recent years on the grounds that their presence on the platform could cause accidents. Model railway engineers, too, have been threatened with extinction thanks to the European Pressure Equipment Directive which places a new inspection regime on the manufacturers of boilers: they must pay to be inspected at a cost of £700 a day. The rules were designed to ensure the safety of workers in factories, but for some reason has also been applied to makers of model trains. In fact, most model trains use copper boilers – which unlike steel boilers deform rather than explode under excessive pressure.

• We might just remember at this point that the EU was responsible for conceiving Value-Added Tax (VAT) which since 1973 has been confusing shopkeepers – and costing the taxpayer a fortune in fraud. According to the EU Tax Commissioner, VAT fraud is costing European governments 50 billion euros (£35 billion) a year. One of the favourite scams is so-called 'carousel' VAT fraud. Goods are shipped into the EU and sold, but without the fraudsters paying a bean in VAT. The goods are then exported from the EU, whereupon VAT is reclaimed from the taxman – even though it was never paid in the first place. Unlike simple tax evasion, where the Government is merely deprived of tax revenue, with carousel fraud the taxpayer actually subsidises the fraudster.

• …And who could forget the Common Agricultural Policy (CAP), which consumes half the EU's £579 billion budget, mostly in the form of huge subsidies to farmers, often to produce food which nobody wants to buy. The result is that agriculture has become completely detached from market forces. Farmers have been reduced to paupers, forever reliant on the charity of the state and forced to use their ingenuity not to market their products but to work their way through the labyrinth of paperwork needed to claim their subsidies. The fastest-growing crop in Europe must be the softwood plantations which are supplying the CAP.

Come to think of it, there is so much red tape entangling the countryside that it is worth a chapter all by itself…

9

THE

COUNTRYSIDE

THIRTY years after the forma-tion of the wine lakes and butter mountains the European Union finally decided that something really must be done about the Common Agricultural Policy (CAP). It decided to 'reform' it – which, given the mixture of stubbornness, bloody-mindedness and blatant nationalism which governs negotiations within the EU, really means that everybody flapped around to find a solution which, so far as the French were concerned, meant that everything could carry on just as before.

So, on 1 May 2005, the reformed CAP came into being. No longer were farmers to be paid for growing vast surpluses  of food that nobody wants. Instead, under the new system, farmers are paid, er, for growing nothing whatsoever. They now qualify for their subsidies simply by keeping their land 'in agricultural condition' – i.e. by dragging a plough over it once a year or by letting a few bedraggled sheep graze on it. No surprise then, that shortly before the new regime came into force British land agents were getting strong interest from wealthy businessmen interested in buying farmland.

And so it came to pass. As soon as the reforms were introduced, the number of 'farmers' in Britain mysteriously increased from 80,000 to 120,000; the extra claimants, it turned out, qualified for payments on the grounds that they possessed small paddocks or allotments, activities which had previously been considered hobbies. Rural homeowners who buy their daughter a pony, for example, may now claim £8 an acre for their paddock land. So many were claiming that the Rural Payments Agency (RPA)— the new quango set up to dispense the money – at one point fell five months behind making payments.

And yet…while the Rural Payments Agency hands out money willy-nilly, a Carlisle man was charged £865 for planning permission to keep a horse in a field. Grazing a horse on agricultural land, he was told, was fine, but he had brought hay onto the field and put one or two jumps on it – and that constituted 'keeping' a horse, which required change-of-use planning permission.

For the taxpayer the only consolation is that farmers have

to jump through so many hoops in order to claim their money that it is possible to feel that by the time they finally get their hands on the cash they have, in a perverse sort of way, earned it. The claims process goes like this:

1. Firstly, the farmer must ring up the Rural Payments Agency and ask for a 24 page SP5a application form.

2. Before he can fill it in he is ordered first to read a 112 page booklet, the Single Payment Scheme: Handbook and Guidance, plus six other documents.

3. He can now fill in the form and send it off.

4. Next, he must apply for a 'holding number' for his land. This involves filling in another 15 page form, accompanied by 40 pages of guidance.

5. Finally, and usually after many months, a cheque will appear in the post.

The people who have benefited most from the new CAP regime are the bureaucrats at the Rural Payments Agency employed to administer it, and who appear to have been having a high old time at their offices at Newcastle-upon-Tyne. In June 2006 the quango started an investigation into allegations that staff had been caught on camera taking drugs, having sex in the lavatories and jumping naked from filing cabinets – the very cabinets, presumably, which contained forms for some of the 58,000 claims still outstanding from a year earlier.

That just about sums up the great racket that is the CAP: farmers filling in forms, bureaucrats frolicking naked and the taxpayer picking up the tab. Why can't we just do away with the subsidies (and the bureaucrats) altogether and let farmers get on with it? That is exactly what happened in New Zealand 20 years ago. The result? Farming is booming – and it doesn't cost the taxpayer a penny.

Needless to say, the vast handouts under CAP are an open invitation to fraud. In 2000, the National Audit Office reported that £700 million worth of fraud and financial irregularities were committed within the EU. For the past 11 years the European Court of Auditors has refused to sign the EU's accounts, on the basis that its £63 billion annual budget has not been properly accounted for. I would call the following some of the most entertaining examples of fraud engendered by the EU's fiscal and regulatory policies – if only it wasn't our money that was being frittered away:

• In 2003 the European Court of Auditors revealed that 50.2 per cent of Portuguese suckler cows do not exist.

• A Greek farmer claimed that 501 of his sheep had been eaten by wolves or died from diseases in two years. Yet he still had 470 sheep left – the same number as when he started, and could provide no evidence that he had restocked his farm.

• A Somerset farmer managed to claim £865,799 of payments under the Agricultural Flat Rate VAT Scheme for trading sheep which did not exist.

• According to subsidy claim forms there is 89.7 per cent more farmland in Luxembourg than actually exists.

The principle aim of the CAP 'reforms' was to prevent the production of vast surpluses of produce which nobody wanted to buy. Now that farmers are no longer paid specifically to produce food, goes the theory, they will be much more responsive to the market, producing only what is in demand.

Alas, no such luck. In 2006, a year after the 'reforms' had been introduced, the European Commission announced that it was going to spend 131 million euros (£90 million) buying 430 million bottles of unwanted French wine and 371 million bottles of Italian wine which would then be distilled into fuel and industrial alcohol. French wine-growers were distraught at the announcement, but not because their fine cuvées and appellations were being turned into paint-stripper. No, what upset them was that they wanted EU taxpayers to buy up 1.1 billion bottles of the stuff, not a measly 430 million.

There's an argument that farmers wouldn't need subsidies if it were not for the absurd number of regulations which now stand in the way of making a living. A Derbyshire dairy farmer talks despairingly of the eight booklets totalling 403 pages of rules which she is annually sent by the Department for Rural Affairs, covering issues from animal welfare to disposal of waste.

Worse, she says, is the bureaucracy involved in the 'Farm Assured' scheme, which is supposed to give consumers confidence that animals are bred to the highest welfare standards. "We have to keep a record for each animal, which, if you do it properly, runs to 10 pages. We have to mark down, from one to ten, how difficult its birth was. We have to record every time it is given treatment. And then we have to keep all this information to show the inspector when he comes round, once a year. Then he just stands there and flicks through it. He doesn't even read it properly. What's the point?"

It must have seemed a fine idea to the DEFRA official who came up with it: let's have a little biography of each cow. I am sure it will be very helpful if cows of the future want to research their family history. But of course, all it achieves in the meantime is to wrap up farmers in paperwork and give them less time to do what they really want to do – look after their animals.

And it isn't just dairy farmers. An EU directive now requires every egg produced in Europe to be stamped with information including the date it was laid and the identity of the chicken. Printers used to stamp eggs cost £5,000; each laying hen, on the other hand, makes its owner a profit of just 50 pence over its lifetime.

The EU Directive on Vibration and Noise at Work threatened to make it illegal to drive a tractor for more than three hours a day. Tough luck if there are thunderstorms approaching and you need to get your hay in before it is flattened.

Under the 'reformed' CAP farmers are encouraged to keep their land in good environmental condition. One of the new rules forbids them from driving heavy machinery – including tractor and plough onto the land if it is waterlogged, in order to protect the soil. A puddle within 20 metres of a gate, farmers have been told, is okay, but a puddle more than 20 metres from a gate constitutes a waterlogged field, ruling out the use of a plough. In other words, farmers are supposed to check with a tape measure every time they want to plough a field. Why can't they be trusted to decide themselves whether the field is too wet?

Under the Badger Protection Act 1992 landowners face severe penalties for tampering with badger sets – which can involve nothing more than poking a stick down one of the entrances. Miscreants can be fined £5,000 or jailed for six months for every animal harmed. Interfere with the sets of 26 badgers, in other words, and you can be jailed for 13 years – the average sentence served by a murderer. And yet by the time the Badger Protection Act was passed badgers were in no danger whatsoever. They were an endangered species in the 1950s, when the original rules protecting them were introduced, but thereafter their numbers increased to an estimated 250,000 in 1987 and 440,000 in 1997 – becoming, in some locations, a pest.

Yet wildlife laws oblige landowners to kill other mammals no more common than the badger. If you catch a mink or a grey squirrel in a trap it is illegal to release it alive. It is hard to square this regulation with another law, passed in 2000, outlawing mink farming on the basis that it is cruel.

These are far from being the only nutty rules and regulations involving animals:

• The law allows you to kill or give away a bullfinch – but not to sell or barter it.

• Farmers and horse-owners have been told that they may no longer keep a pile of dung weighing more than five tonnes unless they first apply for a licence costing between £100 and £500, depending on the weight of dung kept on one site. Just one question: who in their right mind goes around weighing dung piles?

• An EU directive has made it illegal to put kitchen waste on a commercial compost heap, so The National Trust discovered, if the waste comes from a kitchen where meat is prepared. Instead, it has to be taken away as trade waste and disposed, at great cost, in landfill sites.

• Horse owners are now obliged to buy horse passports at a cost of £50 per horse. This is not to allow them to travel – only a miniscule number of horses leave our shores. It is so that a record can be kept of equine drugs – so that, should the knacker's yard sell them to a French butcher, they can safely be consumed by humans. Given this bureaucracy, one might assume that the Government would be happy to classify horses as agricultural animals – thereby making it unnecessary for businesses such as riding schools to pay full business rates. But no, the Government has refused to do this.

• Two fishermen from Scarborough were given a conditional discharge and ordered to pay £300 in costs for selling six lobsters 86mm long. The creatures contravened an EU regulation demanding that lobsters only be caught if they are at least 87mm long.

• Regulation of the fishing industry costs £108 million a

year – for an industry worth £600 million. Every year 4,000 vessels are boarded, 40 per cent of catches are inspected, and fishermen have to fill in 170,000 log sheets.

• South Welsh farmer Stephen Jones was threatened with a £5,000 fine or a six month jail sentence, under the Conservation (Natural Habitats) Regulations 1994 for driving his tractor through a piece of woodland on his way to erect a fence. The Countryside Council of Wales complained that he had damaged a dormouse habitat. Nobody, however, has ever seen a dormouse on the land – though a conservationist once claimed to have seen a hazelnut with toothmarks in it.

A Scottish Farmer who rang the quango Scottish Natural Heritage asking whether he could reintroduce dormice onto his land was threatened with prosecution – under the Dangerous Wild Animals Act. Any reports of a human being savaged by a dormouse will be gratefully received.

• The Food Standards Agency in 2004 floated a proposal to ban the practice of allowing sheep and other animals to graze in orchards, arguing that fruit-eaters risked contracting e-coli from the animals' faeces. It later transpired that the rule was only going to apply to orchards which grew 'ready-to-eat' fruit picked straight from the trees. Bizarrely, the rule was not going to apply to orchards where windfalls were used to make fruit juice and cider – fruits which, unlike those hanging from trees, were actually in danger of being splattered with animal droppings.

But don't let's just blame the EU. That would be lazy – and wrong. In 2001 Britain suffered an outbreak of foot and mouth disease. The Government repeatedly said that it would be illegal to vaccinate animals, preferring to slaughter them instead – and, while it was about it, close down the countryside – driving away tourists who make an even bigger contribution to the economy than do pig, cattle and sheep farmers. It later turned out that the advice was wrong: when foot and mouth spread to Holland, animals were quickly rounded up and vaccinated. Meanwhile, in Britain, the Government achieved:

• The closure of every public footpath in Suffolk and Lincolnshire, in spite of the fact that those counties possess hardly any farm animals, just a lot of wheat and turnip fields.

• The incarceration of the Bishop of Carlisle in his own home, in Dalston, Cumbria – on the basis that sheep in the field next door were infected with the virus. Vets employed by the Ministry of Agriculture, Fisheries and Food, on the other hand, came and went from the field while the bishop was imprisoned next door.

• The cancellation of Crufts, even though dogs are not affected by the disease.

Needless to say, the taxpayer picked up the tab for the incompetence. The Government had to pay compensation for each of the 6.5 million animals destroyed. Remarkably, in spite of the fact that the foot and mouth brought an immediate ban on meat exports, the market price for a carcass seemed to grow dramatically during the outbreak, as farmers learned how to play the system. The final bill to taxpayers was £3 billion, while the tourist industry lost £5 billion, for which it was not compensated.

And has anything been learned from its cumbersome tackling of foot and mouth?

You must be joking. The Government recently suggested

that it was ready to consider restarting a nuclear power station building programme. It has not yet revealed where it intends to put the waste, but presumably it has something in mind. After all, ministers have certainly taken no chances with dead farm animals. Traditionally, farm animals which die unexpectedly have been buried in obscure corners of farms. But all that changed with the Animal By-Products Order (1999), which insists all dead animals be taken to a rendering plant, where they can be reduced to goo. Supposedly this is vital in order to protect the environment. But it does seem to have escaped the notice of bureaucrats that each year millions of birds and wild mammals drop dead in the countryside, and decompose naturally, without ill effect.

Even when dead animals do reach rendering plants, red tape is making it increasingly difficult for animals to be disposed of efficiently. Until recently rendering plants kept going by burning tallow derived from the animals of which they were disposing. Not only did it save energy, it reduced the volume of waste which had to be transported for disposal elsewhere. It worked well; until that is the British Government decided, under an EU directive on waste, that tallow should be officially classified as a waste product. For no reason other than bureaucracy, tallow is now forbidden from being burnt at rendering plants and instead must be driven to licensed waste disposal sites. This will cost rendering plants an extra £70,000 in fuel a year and increase carbon emissions by 750,000 tonnes a year.

And while we are on the subject of waste…that's worth a little chapter all to itself as well…

IO

WASTE

IT isn't just regulations on agricultural waste which are bananas. In 2003, Teeside waste-management company Able UK won a £10.8 million contract to dismantle 13 former US warships which had been sitting at anchor off Virginia. It applied for and received permission from the relevant authority, the Environment Agency, to carry out the work. The ships were duly sailed across the Atlantic, and had nearly reached Hartlepool when Friends of the Earth won a High Court ruling reversing the Environment Agency's permission. Able UK, ruled the court, only had planning permission to dismantle 'marine structures' – which do not include ships. In 2006 the ships were still at anchor off Hartlepool, waiting to be broken up. If they were full of deadly toxins, needless to say, those toxins by now would have leaked out and polluted the sea for miles around.

Many businesses tell a similar story: the laws on waste disposal are now so bureaucratic and contradictory that it is often impossible to do the right thing – other than by sitting on the waste on your own premises. As a result of the EU Hazardous Waste Directive, or perhaps more accurately because of the Government's failure to prepare for the directive, all but 12 waste disposal sites have ceased to accept hazardous waste. In Scotland, not a single site is left – meaning that a manufacturing company in Inverness has to drive its waste all the way to England, with all the potential for spillage which that entails. The landfill tax has provided such an incentive for dishonest tradesmen to dispose of their rubbish illegally that councils in North London in 2003 spent £1 million clearing up 70,000 tonnes of illegally-dumped waste. Yet the landfill tax which would have been collected had the rubbish been legally disposed of was just £135,000.

It isn't just hazardous waste, either. Any trade waste is now treated as if it were radioactive. Disposing of it is horribly expensive for business – though it does create work for council bureaucrats. This, according to one local authority, is what one carpet-fitter, fined for fly-tipping, should have done to dispose of a carpet legally:

"He should have rung us up and we would have sent someone out in a van to inspect the waste. For this service we charge £20 per hour for each person we send, because we might need to send more than one person, and an extra £10 an hour for the van. Then we would have given him a price for disposing of it, which in the case of a carpet would have been £35 per tonne."

Of course he did the wrong thing by dumping the carpet where he did, but when doing the right thing is so complicated and expensive, is it any wonder that the countryside is gradually disappearing under fridge mountains, piles of dumped cars and other rubbish? The situation is about to get worse, too. The introduction of a European directive on electrical goods (the charmingly-named WEEE directive) will make it illegal for consumers to throw electrical items into their dustbin. Instead, they will have to return them to designated collection points, where the manufacturers of the goods will be obliged to take them back and recycle what they can. In its aims the directive has a perfectly noble purpose, but what the legislators cannot appear to see is that many idle consumers will not be bothered to return their electrical goods to a collection point – which, if the provision of hazardous waste sites is anything to go by, will be few and far between. They will simply dump them in the nearest hedge. What the new rules lack is any kind of incentive structure: how about a deposit on electrical goods which, like the deposit on lemonade bottles 30 years ago, is returned to the customer when the item is traded in?

Then, old electrical goods would have a value and there would be a financial incentive not to dump them.

Many of the dumped goods end up having to be disposed of at the landowner's expense. The only good news for a farmer who wakes up to a pile of old fridges on his land is that it won't stop him claiming his agricultural subsidies... Under the 'reformed' CAP a crop of fridges counts every bit as much as a crop of barley.

By the way: we haven't even dealt with recycling yet...

Recycling is all the rage. Under the EU recycling directive, by 2015 one third of Britain's domestic waste will have to be recycled. In order to meet this target local authorities have busily been introducing recycling boxes for paper, glass, plastics and many other things. The response of the public has been highly worthy: most householders have quickly adopted the habit each week of sorting out their rubbish into different boxes.

The waste is then collected, sorted and – well, after all that effort, quite a lot of it seems never actually to be recycled. Conscientious homeowners in 2005 carefully sorted out millions of coloured glass bottles for recycling collections – 190,000 tonnes of which failed to find any sort of buyer. By 2008, there will be 500,000 tonnes of coloured glass sitting in depots across the country – because there is no market for coloured recycled glass.

One third of the paper and plastic collected in recycling bins in Britain is sold to plants in China – where, it has subsequently been revealed – very few records are kept of what actually happens to it. According to Dutch customs officials who seized a 1,000 tonne consignment of British waste 'paper' after it was discovered to contain plastic bottles and all sorts of rubbish, much of the waste sold to the third world for recycling is being traded illegally. Are we spending hours sorting out our rubbish, paying to have it carted halfway around the world, with all the carbon emissions that entails, to have it burned and buried in China instead? We don't know. No audit of the environmental benefits of recycling has ever been produced – it is simply taken as a given that recycling is a good in itself.

The recycling targets sit awkwardly with another target which has been set by the Government: that 10 per cent of all our energy must come from renewable sources. One way to meet this target would be to build 'combined heat and power' (CHP) plants close to our towns. In a CHP plant rubbish is burned, and the heat used to generate electricity. The heat which cannot be turned into electricity is pumped, in the form of hot water, to nearby homes – making this a highly-efficient way to get rid of rubbish and to provide energy. Moreover, large incinerators can operate at extremely high temperatures, ensuring efficient burning and little pollution.

Unfortunately, however, there is just one thing standing in the way of building CHP plants: the target insisting that one third of our rubbish must be recycled.

(Just another bit of silliness: in 2006 the Health and Safety Executive spent three months and goodness knows how many million on a risk assessment of recycling collections and concluded that the standard 55 litre recycling boxes used by local authorities could be damaging our backs. It has recommended authorities issue 40 litre boxes instead. Councils will now have to consign millions of black plastic boxes to the waste tip in order to meet with the approval of the HSE.)

Visitors to the English countryside in the early months of 2002 would have noticed a strange new crop in the fields, not to mention lay-bys, recreation grounds and pieces of woodland. It was the white hulks of illegally-dumped fridges. Remarkably, this ugly and poisonous residue was the result of an EU directive designed to protect the environment. In 1999 the EU decided that as from 1 January 2002, disused fridges must not be scrapped until they have had all foam pumped out of them. In itself, this was a reasonable enough new regulation – except that officials at the then Department for Environment, Food and Rural Affairs forgot to tell the Environment Agency until 19 November 2001 – just six weeks before the new law was to come into effect. The result was that by the time the deadline passed there was not a single plant in the UK capable of pumping out the foam and disposing of it in the approved way. It therefore became impossible to scrap a fridge legally – all that could be done was to store the fridges until the specialist equipment became available. At one point fridges were piling up at the rate of 6,500 a week.

And yet when the Government comes across an inspired example of recycling which it did not itself instigate…

For years the asphalt industry has been doing the environment a favour by using as a raw material the four million litres of waste oil every week removed from the sumps of British vehicles. The practice provided a means of disposing of the oil – and reduced the consumption of new oil. Until, that is, the European Directive on Waste Incineration classified oil as 'waste' – which could only be disposed of in hazardous waste sites.

Doug Hilton has done his bit for the environment by turning an ugly chalk quarry into a wetland nature reserve, using £360,000 of his own money. Having attracted kingfishers, swans and geese, he wanted to build some islands for the birds and construct a path around his lake, using uncontaminated waste material from the construction industry. What he hadn't reckoned with was the Water Resources Act, under which he is required to pay landfill tax on any material dumped into water. The bill, for finding an imaginative way of disposing of waste other than in an unsightly waste tip? A whopping £2.5 million.

That just about sums up everything that is wrong with the bureaucratic mind. Think of a noble aim: we must cut the amount of waste being dumped in waste tips. Come up with a solution which appears to lead in the right direction: a tax which discourages people to dump rubbish in landfill sites. Then enforce it in such a pedantic fashion that it ends up achieving exactly the opposite of what you set out to achieve.

It is the same with the planning rules by which the Government seeks to build 70 per cent of all new homes on previously-developed, or 'brownfield' land. In August 2006 the Government proudly declared, to loud cheers of self-congratulation, that it had reached its target. A great boon for the countryside? Hardly. Here are two reasons why this was purely a bureaucratic achievement:

1. The back gardens of suburban villas are mysteriously classified as 'brownfield' sites (yet an old ironstone quarry in Corby counted as a greenfield site).

2. While over 70 per cent of new homes were built on brownfield land, no corresponding target was set for commercial development. So what local authorities were doing to achieve their targets was creating zones for new housing on the sites of old shops, offices and factories – and relocating these developments to greenfield sites. In other words thousands of British homeowners are now living on the poisoned sites of old gas works – and then going out to work in office parks on the fringes of lush open countryside. Commonsense suggests that it ought to be the other way round.

II

THOU SHALT NOT HAVE FUN

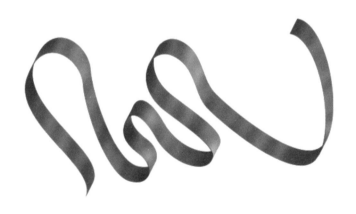

L AST summer I visited a zoo in Northern Spain. It was a thoroughly modern institution. No animal in its care, to paraphrase the Geneva Convention on prisoners of war, was allowed to be treated to cruel or unusual punishment; nor, for that matter, be made the subject of public curiosity. Instead, the animals, in keeping with current thought, were encouraged to 'express natural behaviour' well away from view of the paying visitors. To this end the bears had been provided with an enclosure which measured half a square mile, its chain link perimeter fence concealing a sylvan paradise of trees and bushes. Anxious to catch sight of an animal, my son and I followed the fence for over a mile, watching for signs of twitching undergrowth. Would we catch a fleeting glimpse of one of these magnificent creatures, or would they prove elusive, as they hunted and gathered their supper deep in the bush?

For half an hour we saw nothing. We should have guessed. The bears turned out all to be gathered down by the car park where they were rolling in the dirt, rubbing their bellies, standing on two legs and generally entertaining a grateful public. Natural behaviour, evidently the bears had decided, is boring. They wanted to entertain.

Sadly, that is a pleasure which ever fewer animals are being allowed to indulge. Animals have all but been driven out of the circus. Moreover, zoos are no longer allowed simply to be zoos. Under EU directive 1999/22/EC keeping animals for public entertainment is only allowed so long as your zoo is prepared 'to become involved more directly in the conservation of biodiversity through educational projects of benefit to the conservation of species and by participating in measures such as breeding and research'.

The obsession with animal welfare knows few bounds. In the 18th century Britain gave the world Thomas Paine's the Rights of Man. What has Tony Blair's government given the world? The Rights of Goldfish. In what must surely rank as one of the most important breakthroughs for justice for many decades, the Government has come up with a proposal to prohibit goldfish being presented as fairground prizes.

And the Rights of Pigs... A group of gas customers protesting about excessive profits made by their suppliers wanted to take a 40 stone sow, Winnie, to accompany them on a publicity stunt outside the AGM of the gas company

Centrica. They soon discovered that there was another breed of fat cat living off their hard-earned money: state bureaucrats. They abandoned plans to take Winnie with them after Birmingham City Council ruled that she required something called an 'animal welfare licence'. The protest, it ruled, constituted a public performance and would infringe the animal's dignity. In fact, all Winnie was going to be required to do was to consume a bucket of swill in front of the cameras: a treat which she missed out on.

Circuses, like zoos, have been legislated within an inch of their lives in recent years. From 2005 they have been required to obtain a public entertainment licence – not just once but in every place they perform. Worse, the licences cost up to £500 a time. Given that a circus on tour can visit as many as 40 towns, that means a bill of £20,000 before a single employee has been paid.

And it isn't just animals which miss out in the Government's great crusade against fun…

Among the little known provisions of the Royal Parks Regulations (1997), which cover Hyde Park, Regents Park and most other big London parks, are the following prohibitions.

> Thou shalt not:
> Play a musical instrument
> Dip your toe into a fountain
> Use any 'mechanically-propelled toy or 'any foot-propelled device'
> Feed a pelican
> 'Interfere with any plant or fungus' – such as, presumably, by making a daisy chain.

A few more things you can't do any more...

• The British Beer and Pub Association has counted 20 signs which pubs are now expected to display for the 'benefit' of their customers, warning people not to smoke at the bar, to look out for thieves, drink-spikers, rapists, drink-drivers, foods which cause allergies. And that is before we have even got to the European proposal to put health warnings on the booze itself...

• The signs on the roads entering Bury St Edmunds in Suffolk proudly declare it to be 'Britain's Floral Town'.

With that in mind, shoe shop-owner Kate Palliser thought she would enter into the spirit of it by displaying some pink camellias and a few Union Jacks to celebrate the Queen's 80th birthday. The council immediately ordered her to take them down, on the grounds they were obstructing the public highway and a danger to the public. If anyone knows of somebody who has had their eye gouged out in an accident involving a camellia, would they please get in touch?

• 52 year old grandmother Suzanne Hansford was trying to take photographs of her four year old granddaughter in a Southampton paddling pool when she was warned by a council employee that a by-law prohibited it – the council couldn't be sure she wouldn't post the pictures on a paedophile website. Nice to know that the authorities have a sense of proportion about the fear of paedophiles. When confronted with a real paedophile – Craig Sweeney, convicted in 2003 for the sexual assault of a six year old girl – the courts released him after just 15 months. He promptly drove to Wales, abducted a three year old girl, drove her down the M4, assaulted her – and was given another jail sentence, this one which could allow him to be released in five years' time. Okay, the courts got it wrong first time round, but as long as they are keeping an eye on those white-haired grannies hanging round paddling pools with their grand-daughters, at least we know they are doing something.

There are many unpleasant realities in modern Britain: drugs, alcohol, gambling. But I am not sure that out of the Hogarthian nightmare that has descended upon some of our inner cities and town centres many people would necessarily identify one particular social ill: the excessive size of some of the teddy bears given as fairground prizes. The Government thinks otherwise. One of the proposals in the gambling bill, as originally presented to the House of Commons in 2004, was a clause to limit the value of teddy bear prizes from £8 to £5. Children who won too large a teddy bear, went the argument, might be tempted into a gambling habit later in life.

Actually, come to think of it, the limitation of teddy bears from £8 to £5 just about wins the prize for the most pathetic regulation introduced by the Blair government. Presumably the fairgrounds of Britain are now 'swept' daily by plain clothes teddy-bear police assessing the value of every stuffed toy on offer. "What do you think of that one, Sarge? Those swivelling eyes must push it way over the £5 mark."

No, hang on a minute: that is far too straightforward.

What the Government really needs is a Teddy Bear Valuation Agency (TBVA), which employs half the population of a small northern town and to which fairground operators must submit a 112 page form for every soft toy they wish to give away as a prize, detailing the quality of the fur, the size of the ears and so on – which then gets stashed away in a filing cabinet while staff watch porn on their computers, frolic naked with confiscated teddies and blame backlogs on 'understaffing'.

While the nation's children have been saved from the evil influence of oversize teddy bears, let no-one say the Government has not also achieved some deregulation. Thanks to the new gambling and drinking laws…residents' lives are now made a misery by 24 hour drinking. And there will soon be a network of super-casinos where the poor can go and fritter away their welfare benefits.

But at least citizens need no longer live in fear of certain dangerous practices. The following things have been reported to be banned in at least one school:

- Making daisy chains (risk of picking up germs)
- Playing hopscotch (risk of injury)
- Playing football (encourages competitiveness)
- Wearing hair gel (fire risk)

- Making anything out of egg boxes (fear of salmonella)
- Home-made cakes (might contain e-coli)
- Putting hands up (makes pupils who don't have the answers feel victimised)
- Parents taking photographs of their – fully clothed – children in school plays (the photographs might fall into the hands of paedophiles)
- Wearing a plastercast (other children might fall over it)
- Wearing flared trousers (children might trip up)
- Removing sweatshirts – even in 85 degree heat (children might suffer sunburn)
- Throwing paper aeroplanes (might cause eye injuries)
- Girls wearing skirts (which might make them too attractive to drooling old men passing the school – they were ordered to wear trousers instead)

Needless to say, the nannying doesn't stop when children go home. Ofcom, the regulatory body for the television industry, has banned advertisers using pop stars, film stars and other celebrities from appearing in any food advert aimed at the under 10s. What, even if they are advertising oranges? It would seem so.

It is a principle of a free society that anything not specifically banned by statute is deemed to be legal. On this basis a free-born Briton – by my reckoning, though somebody may well correct me – may still:

- Sing in the bath (so long as they do not exceed 35 decibels if after 11pm)

- Sit on a tuffet and eat curds and whey (so long as the tuffet does not conceal a badger set and you don't try to pass off the curds and whey as Feta cheese, which must be manufactured in Greece).

- Call the Prime Minister a twerp (though not within a kilometre of Westminster, where it would constitute a political protest, requiring permission from the Commissioner of the Metropolitan Police, and as long as you don't put it on a tee-shirt and wear it in public, where it might cause distress).

- And finally, lest somebody tell you that the Government has banned absolutely everything, there is one thing it has actually legalised: having sex in a public lavatory – so long, that is, according to Hilary Benn when introducing the Sex Offences bill, you take the trouble to close the door first.

12

WORK

Work is the curse of the Drinking Classes
Oscar Wilde

O SCAR Wilde's famous dictum has become official Government policy. Thanks to changes in the licensing laws, British workers are now free to drink in bars 24 hours a day. But work? By God, no. It might harm them.

Among the lunatic rules imposed to stop people from working:

• An accountant at the Contributions Agency was forced to retire from his job at the age of just 60. Allowing him to work for longer, ruled his employers, would have been injurious to his health – even though non-public sector workers cannot collect their pensions until the age of 65. The worker concerned was more worried about the effect on his health of not being able to work: a picture of bounding energy, he had recently sired a daughter and was worried that he would not have enough money to bring her up.

In spite of blatantly forcing its own employees to retire at 60 against their will the Government has brought in legislation, to take effect on 1 December 2006, to prevent age discrimination in private industry. Among the things which employers are warned could land them in hot water are:

• Asking for an applicant's age on a job application form (even though the company will have to find out somehow because, should they be employed, Her Majesty's Revenue and Customs will demand to know).

• Write such things as 'candidate shows remarkable maturity for his age' on an assessment of performance (presumably employers are now expected to believe that spotty 18 year olds fresh from school possess as much wisdom as those who have spent a lifetime in the workplace).

• Advertise a vacancy only in a newspaper whose readership profile is weighted towards the young. Fortunately, this should have one beneficial effect: it will mean that Government departments and quangos will no longer be able to advertise public sector jobs solely in *The Guardian*.

• Call a colleague 'the postroom boy', on the grounds that other employees might think this is a job only suitable for the young.

The regulations protecting employees against unfair dismissal are now so onerous that they are acting as a brake on job creation. But again, it is one law for the Government and another for the rest of us. Under the statutory dismissal, disciplinary and grievance procedures introduced in 2004, any employer wanting to sack an ineffective or dishonest employee must go through a five stage procedure:

1. A verbal warning
2. A written warning
3. Another written warning, this time inviting the employee to a meeting
4. A face-to-face meeting, along to which the employee is entitled to bring a colleague or trade union official
5. The employee can now be dismissed, but only pending an appeal

Yet again, this is a regulation from which the Government sees fit to excuse itself. On 5 May 2006, the Prime Minister, Tony Blair, conducted a reshuffle of his cabinet. Several ministers were sacked, others demoted – all in the space of a few hours. Remarkably, there is no sign that any of the above procedures were carried out. Rather, Mr

Blair made up his mind who was going to be sacked, summoned them to Downing Street and summarily dismissed them. Sadly, those dismissed were too much party toadies to complain to an employment tribunal – otherwise it might have been rather interesting.

It is not merely difficult to sack employees these days; in some cases firms are forced to employ workers whom they do not need and do not wish to employ. Under the Transfer of Undertakings (Protection of Employment) Regulations, companies which take over contracts previously held by other companies can in certain circumstances be forced to take on many of the staff already doing the job. In one case a Suffolk distribution company was forced to take on staff at a cost of £550,000. This rather defeats the purpose of putting contracts out for tender: what if the inefficiency of the previous contractors was down to lazy staff? What is there to be gained if the same old lazy staff are still going to be doing the job, albeit under new management?

The Working Time Regulations provide another example of one rule for our leaders, one rule for the rest of us. How many times have you read about ministers and officials 'working through the night' to stitch together a deal on the latest piece of pettifogging EU regulation? It ought not to be possible for ministers to do this: under the EU Working

Time Directive, workers are not supposed to put in more than 48 hours a week nor work continuously for more than 11 hours a day. Having finished their photocall and their working dinner, EU negotiators ought to knock off for the day, leaving their business incomplete.

If only they would. The rest of us would certainly be better off. When the Working Time Regulations were passed in Britain in 1998 they came with an important opt-out: employees could overlook the maximum 48 hour week if they personally signed an agreement saying they were prepared to work longer. Moreover, workers were exempt from the legislation in cases where their working time 'is partly unmeasured or determined by the worker himself'. There was a very clear reason for this: if you work in a baked bean factory it is very easy to distinguish between the time you are at work and the time you are off-duty. If you are a senior manager, on the other hand, your day almost certainly consists of a series of working breakfasts, train journeys accompanied by laptops and supper interrupted by important calls.

However, an amendment to the regulations in 2006 removed this exemption: henceforth, people who run their own businesses are obliged formally to sign – with themselves – an agreement to work longer hours. Moreover, they must now keep a log of how many hours they are

actually working. What about the time one spends in the bath, contemplating whether to expand into Belgium: does that now count as working time or not? When John Prescott was photographed in May 2006 wielding a croquet mallet on the lawns of Dorneywood, his former official residence, he complained bitterly that he was actually holding a working meeting at the time. He probably was. Presumably, he entered it all in the official log of his working hours – taking care to distinguish the time which he spent actually hitting the ball, from the time he spent talking business between hoops. Or maybe not. One doesn't, of course, expect ministers to obey their own pettifogging rules.

All that the new regulations achieve is to make sure that businessmen work even longer hours than they did before – on the non-productive task of totting up their hours. And to what point? When the French introduced a compulsory 35 hour week the productivity per hour of French workers shot up. Yet productivity per man stayed the same. Were French workers really producing the same in fewer hours at work – or did French businesses suddenly have an incentive to fib about the number of hours they are working?

The Work and Families Act 2006 extends the rights of fathers to paternity leave, and for the first time allows mothers to switch their maternity leave to their partners. Having spent much of the past decade trying to remove mothers with new babies from the workplace, the Government now seems intent in getting them back to work. The 2006 Act obliges companies to allow mothers on maternity leave to return for occasional 'Keeping in Touch Days' – even though the company is paying somebody else to do their job while they are on maternity leave.

And if you thought you could escape the monster of red tape by setting up in business on your own...

Butchers' shops which sell non-meat products alongside meat products – even if it is just the odd packet of stuffing to go with a turkey – now have to apply for an annual licence costing £100. All butchers' shops are regularly inspected by health and safety officers trained to spot such dangers as blood dripping over a display of tomatoes – so why the need for the extra licence?

The new Licensing Act was sold to the public as a deregulatory measure, which would make it easier for them to get a drink when they wanted one – "who gives a XXXX for closing time?" as Labour put its policy in a text message sent to young voters before the 2001 election. But it has not turned out to be quite such a benign piece of deregulation for one Blackpool hotel owner. Her hotel contains a small cocktail bar open only to residents, through which she sells £90 worth of canned beer a year. Before the new act she had to make a simple application every four years for a licence to sell intoxicating liquors – a process which cost £30. Now, she has to fill in four forms, one of them 21 pages long. It costs her £190 a year for a premises licence and £37 every ten years for a personal licence. Furthermore, she must draw a plan of her bar and provide photographs of herself which have been authenticated by a solicitor – all in order to sell £90 worth of beer a year.

A London man closed down the small champagne-importing company which he ran from the back room of his suburban home for the same reason – the bureaucracy entirely wiped out his profits. In addition to filling in the forms he was asked to go on a course showing him how to throw a drunk out of a bar – in spite of the fact that he didn't have a bar and customers never visited him on the premises.

It is hard to think of a single minister in the Labour Government of 1997 to the present day who has any experience in the private sector, let alone run their own business. And it shows. Regulations are coined without any thought to their consequences in terms of lost productivity. For every businessman life has become a constant struggle to balance the time spent breaking through red tape – and time spent doing things which actually earn money.

One of the many burdens on business is supplying data to the Office of National Statistics so that it can compile statistics on – among other things – the productivity of industry. Strangely it seems not to have appreciated that one of the downward pressures on productivity is filling in official forms.

A Norfolk engineering firm was sent a 13 page 'Annual Business Inquiry Form' which the boss was obliged to fill in under pain of a stiff fine under section 4 of the Statistics of Trade Act. Among the statistics he was ordered to supply was 'the total net value of finished work of a capital nature carried out by your own staff produced for your own use. If this value is more than half of total acquisitions, please give an explanation'. In other words, the boss was expected to have noted down the value of every tool made by a toolmaker and the value of every repair performed by a computer systems engineer – all for the benefit of Government statisticians.

I got one too: the Office of National Statistic sent me a long form asking me about my attitudes towards bankrupts. Did I think that bankruptcy still carried a stigma? Did I think it should be made easier for bankrupts to make a fresh start in business? I had better fill in this form, I was warned, or I would face a stiff fine. Presumably the object was to make me bankrupt so that I would be able to fill in the form with the benefit of personal experience.

Then there is the question of where you can work...

The Government has been very keen to persuade more of us to work at home, the argument being that it leads to less traffic congestion. Why, then, punish those who work at home by charging them business rates on their office? The Valuation Office has warned people who work at home that they may be required to pay business rates on a room in which they work – even if it is clearly not self-contained and could not possibly be let as office premises separate from the house.

But it is no better if you rent a dedicated workspace. Employees at a Sussex manufacturing company were forbidden from entering their offices in the middle of the night, on the grounds that the industrial estate on which they were based was only to be used in daytime. No manufacturing was going on during the night – the company simply wanted to be able to do business with its customers in Japan, whose working hours coincide with our night-time.

The mountain of new regulations has stopped many workers working, but at least there is still something they can do: manage. Even the lowliest lavatory-cleaner must by law now be offered a role to play. Under the Information and Consultation of Employees Regulations, companies with more than 150 employees must now by law set up a formal consultation to discuss such things as changes in strategy or mergers and acquisitions. How a floor-sweeper is supposed to come up with anything sensible to say on his bank's proposed merger with a foreign competitor is hard to say.

There is, however, a downside: given the rules on insider-trading, a lowly employee with a few bonus shares could find himself in jail if he inadvertently trades those shares after a consultation on his company's merger.

After falling steadily for several years in 2005 unemployment suddenly began to rise again. Could that just have something to do with ever-more onerous employment legislation which is putting businesses off taking on new staff? Besides the duty not to discriminate, the obligation to set aside prayer rooms, the duty to paternity and maternity leave, don't think an employer's obligations end the day the member of staff walks off with his gold watch. Once you become an employer the state will never let you go – at least not in the time it takes Rip Van Winkle to have 40 winks. One employer was sent the following warning by his insurers:

"Your certificate of Employers' Liability Insurance is attached. The Employers' Liability (Compulsory Insurance) Regulations 1998 require you to keep this certificate or a copy for 40 years."

Is the Government being advised by a manufacturer of filing cabinets, or what?

13

CRIME

ONE evening in 2003 I returned to my car, parked in a Cambridge street, to find that the window on the driver's side had been smashed. Amid the broken glass which covered the seats was a small card. I picked it up and realised that it was the calling card of a policeman. Would I please, as soon as was convenient, please ring the incident room at the local police station.

Could it be, I wondered, that the police officer had spotted the miscreant in the process of committing the offence? No such luck. When I rang the number the officer offered his commiserations, then got down to business. Firstly, would I like some counselling? And secondly, what was my ethnic group?

My what? Yes, I'm sorry about this, the officer replied, almost apologetically, but we have to ask, you understand. Soon it dawned on me: I had been invited to ring the Police not because they had any information to offer, nor that they were actively engaged in searching for the culprit, but because they had some trifling ethnic monitoring form to fill in. And in order to complete it they needed to contact a few crime victims.

That, needless to say, is the mere tip of an iceberg – or rather, paperberg. Police and paperwork have become so synonymous that no political party may now go to the polls without inserting a paragraph along the lines of 'we will free the police from red tape in order to allow them to tackle crime'. Needless to say, the election over, the party in power lets the Home Office get on with designing even bigger and better forms for police officers to fill in.

In a lobby briefing in 2001 the Prime Minister's official spokesman admitted that the Police were spending 40 per cent of their time on paperwork – and only 17 per cent patrolling the streets. The answer? Almost immediately, the Government introduced ethnic monitoring – obliging the Police to collect the information described above. The result will be, presumably, that come the end of the year if a police force has not arrested enough, say, Chinese to fill its annual quota it will have to march down to Chinatown at once and march a few suspects into the station.

A study by Tayside Police revealed that officers had at their disposal an astonishing total of 1,150 different forms. Of these, 112 were regularly used and, on closer analysis, a mere 30 were considered to be necessary. The Home Office regularly announces a crackdown on police red tape – recently claiming to have eliminated 7,700 unnecessary forms – a figure which merely makes one wonder how many there are left. Among the forms to go was a stolen vehicle report form which asked the owner of the lost vehicle to supply a plethora of detail about the car's colour, engine size, level of trim and so on – information which is already on the DVLA's computer system, freely available to the Police. Another was the Prisoner Escort Record form – an A3 size form which recorded medical and other details of every prisoner in the event of the prisoner being transferred to another Police force. In fact, it transpired that only 20 per cent of prisoners are ever transferred to another force, making it superfluous in the remaining 80 per cent of cases.

The elimination of individual forms seems to have made little difference, however. The nation's Plods are still just as buried in paperwork as they were before – particularly on the business of gathering statistics for the benefit of the Government's target-setters. A study by the Metropolitan Police revealed that in 2004/05 the force had spent £101.9 million – 4 per cent of its total budget – on 'non incident-related paperwork' – i.e. absolutely nothing connected with investigating individual crimes. By contrast the Met had spend £62.2 million investigating robberies and £42.2

million investigating house burglaries.

In 2003 the Government set up a new quango called the Assets Recovery Agency, charged with the task of extracting the proceeds of crime from the clutches of criminals. It has not been a noted success. In 2005/06 the agency succeeded in recovering £4.3 million worth of ill-gotten gains. Unfortunately, this was dwarfed by the £18 million which it cost to run the agency.

The Government's excuse for the agency's poor performance is that criminals have successfully been holding up investigations by claiming that their human rights are being infringed. But then this is the same government which introduced the Human Rights Act, making this defence possible. Talk about being hoist on your own petard.

When the Human Rights Act was introduced in 2000 several Government ministers were lined up to herald this great new era of enlightened law-making. They entirely ignored a few sage voices in the House of Lords, notably Lord McCluskey, Scottish judge and vice-chairman of the Human Rights Institute of the International Bar Association, who warned that the act would prove to be "a field day for crackpots, a pain in the neck for judges and a goldmine for lawyers". It took a couple of years for ministers to wonder whether the Human Rights Act was really such a good idea after all. They have spent the rest of their time in office berating the rulings of the courts under the Human Rights Act.

These are a few of the Act's great achievements:

• Anthony Rice, imprisoned on charges of rape and indecent assault, was freed early from prison on licence because probation officers feared that to keep him behind bars would have infringed his human rights. He promptly went out and raped and murdered another woman.

• Nine Afghan asylum-seekers who hijacked a plane on an internal flight and had it diverted to Stansted Airport were allowed to remain in Britain, on the grounds that it would breach their human rights to be sent home to a country where they might suffer torture or murder. But hang on a minute, didn't we invade Afghanistan in 2001 specifically in order to remove the murderers or torturers – namely the Taliban – from power? If it is still impossible to return prisoners to Afghanistan on the grounds they will be ill-treated, it doesn't say much for the achievements of that military campaign. Meanwhile, hijackers around the world have no doubt taken note of the Afghans' experience: hijacking pays. Needless to say, taxpayers were made to foot the bill for their legal costs.

• The serial killer Dennis Nilsen won a case allowing him to look at hardcore pornographic magazines in his cell. He successfully argued that the existing rules, which allowed him only to look at softcore porn magazines, infringed his human rights.

• A convicted arsonist from Lancashire escaped a court order preventing her from carrying a cigarette lighter in public. Her lawyers successfully argued that the order would have prevented her smoking, and therefore would have infringed her human right to free expression.

• A 12 year old Devon schoolboy was given the right to attend school with his hair dyed bright red after his parents threatened to sue the school under the right to free expression.

The point about the Human Rights Act is that it reduces the law to a set of vague principles, and by doing so transfers power from elected politicians. Given the record of the Government in drafting poor legislation there may be something to be said for this. But then at least the public get the chance – occasionally – to harangue politicians for their idiocies. Judges, on the other hand, are unaccountable to the public. It isn't just judges, either, who have been handed the power to invent laws of their choosing. One of the great crime-fighting 'achievements' of the Labour government has been the Anti-Social Behaviour Disorder, or 'Asbo'. This is a device which allows magistrates to bar individuals from particular forms of behaviour – such as drinking in public. In effect the orders allow the courts to invent criminal offences at whim. If the individual breaks the ASBO he can be sent to prison for up to five years.

Nothing quite sums up the lunacy of modern law-enforcement as the following ASBOs:

• A warehouseman from West Lothian was given an ASBO preventing him from watching the film *An American Werewolf in London*, jumping off his sofa and howling.

• A Bristol publican was given an ASBO forcing him to remove a sign from his car park saying 'the Porking Yard', and not to erect any other sign containing the word 'pork'.

It was deemed to offend muslims, who worship in a nearby mosque. But if the worshippers were upset by the presence of the word 'pork' in the vicinity, why did they build their mosque in a street which has a pork butcher, who, happily, has not yet been served with an ASBO?

• A Teeside man received an ASBO preventing him from sniffing petrol on any filling station forecourt in Middlesbrough – but not for some reason on garage forecourts in neighbouring Durham or North Yorkshire.

• A suicidal Bristol woman had an ASBO preventing her from throwing herself into any river or onto any railway line. She was quite welcome, on the other hand, to throw herself into seas, lakes and onto busy roads. One forsees, should she be pulled dripping wet from the Bristol Channel, several days of learned argument as to whether, at the exact point of her immersion, the estuary constituted a river or the open sea.

• A woman from Kilbride was given an ASBO forbidding her from answering the door in her underwear.

• A Manchester car thief received an ASBO forbidding

him from walking or cycling anywhere in the city unless accompanied by his mother or sister. Curiously, it did not specifically ban him from driving or stealing cars. In fact, given that he was banned from walking or cycling about his home city, the ASBO did appear to leave him only one option: to nick a car.

But at least the real criminals are being caught...

A 14 year old Cambridgeshire schoolgirl who 'pinged' the bra of a classmate in an argument over who wore the biggest bra was arrested, finger-printed, had her DNA sampled and was charged with common assault 'of a sexual nature'. Eventually, magistrates gave the girl a complete discharge, asking why the case had come to court in the first place. There is a straightforward answer: it is easier for the Police to tackle this sort of case, and achieve a 'successful' outcome (and thus help meet their targets) than it is to track down real criminals who actually do society some harm.

Jean Grove of Bursledon, Hampshire, was ordered by Police to remove a sign from her front gate reading "Our dogs are fed on Jehovah's Witnesses" – on the grounds that it was offensive. As if to prove that petty policing is a recent phenomenon, the sign had been on Mrs Grove's gate since her late husband erected it after a visit by Jehovah's

Witnesses on Christmas Day 1974. The Police had never complained before: in fact they had once helped find the sign after it had been stolen.

Andy Tierney of Hinckley, Leicestershire, was sent a fixed penalty notice by his local council for £50. His crime? To have dropped two items of litter – into a litter bin. Leaving his home one morning he had bumped into the postman, who handed him two items of junk mail. Not wanting to waste time, he put the unwanted items in a litter bin down the street on his way to work. He was fined under section 87 of the Environmental Protection Act 1990, which prohibits the deposit of domestic refuse in street litter bins.

What about fining the Royal Mail for dumping junk mail on Mr Tierney in the first place? After all, companies which send unsolicited 'spam' emails are threatened with prosecution, so why not companies which deliver junk mail? Oddly enough, the Government sees no reason to extend the laws on email spam to junk mail – in fact, the Royal Mail recently lifted its rule on delivering no more than three plain, unaddressed items of junk mail per house per week, opening the floodgates to junk mail. Could the inconsistency have anything to do with the fact that the Royal Mail is a state-owned company, and therefore the Government has a vested interest in the junk mail industry?

in an attempt to drum up more business. As the YHA manager, Toni Wyatt says: "There are a lot of teachers who are getting to the point of retiring, and younger teachers are finding the whole business of organising a school trip is a pretty scary thing. It is the sheer workload. They have to fill in risk assessments, and get them spot-on."

While genuine abuse continues, often in situations beyond the reach of social services, innocent social interaction between adults and children has come to be conducted like something out of a Carry On film. While presenting a 10 year old girl a prize at a Staffordshire School in 2006 the Reverend Alan Barrett, a Governor of the school, stooped down to give the girl a peck on the cheek. Naturally, as has become common practice these days, social services and the police swooped to conduct an investigation. They concluded that the Reverend had done nothing wrong: his kiss was an innocent gesture and that was that. That was not that, however, as far as the Diocese of Lichfield was concerned. It demanded the vicar resign as a school Governor.

And if you thought it couldn't get any sillier…

Visitors to the Calderdale Royal Hospital in Halifax were asked not to coo at, stare at or ask too many questions of newborn babies in the maternity unit – on the grounds that it could infringe the babies' right to privacy. A manager for the hospital said: "sometimes people touch or talk about the baby like they would if they were examining tins in a supermarket, and that should not happen."

While the Government spends most of its time stopping children doing things, it does occasionally attempt to help them. Not, it has to be said, with a great deal of effect. Founded in the early 1990s, the Child Support Agency (CSA) was supposed to do away with a great iniquity: the tendency of some fathers to walk away from their wives and children, without paying a bean in maintenance. Why should taxpayers support single parents, went the argument, when it should be the duty of absent fathers?

From this noble aim has grown just about the most inefficient public body Britain has ever known. In June 2006 the House of Commons Public Accounts Committee reported that for every £1 of child maintenance which the CSA collects, it spends 70 pence in administrations costs. There is a backlog of 300,000 cases and there is £3.5 billion of uncollected maintenance. As is so often the case with Government red tape, an IT system lies at the heart of the problem. According to the Public Accounts Committee, £800 million had been spent over the previous three years restructuring the agency and installing a new computer system. The computer system turned out to have 500 faults.

Among those parents who have lost out due to the bungling is Jacqueline Harthill, who split up with her husband when her daughter was six months old. After 11 years of dealing with the Child Support Agency she finally received her first tranche of child maintenance: the princely sum of £119.

Some good news: in July 2006 the Government announced that it was going to abolish the Child Support Agency – or rather replace it with a 'slimmed down' agency. We await developments with interest, but experience suggests that the new, leaner and meaner agency will grow even fatter and more pointless than the CSA.

In the meantime, there will be plenty of work for former CSA staff, compiling the Government's proposed £241 million Children's Index – a new database to bring together all sorts of information on the nation's children, and which will be made available to 400,000 doctors, social workers and other officers of the state. The database will include health records, truancy records, exam results and any other information considered relevant to nosey social workers – sorry, relevant to the child's welfare. Each child will have warning flags added to his record, so that as soon as he has received two warning flags an investigation can automatically be launched.

In other words in modern Britain you are not allowed to coo at babies for fear of invading their privacy – but it is absolutely fine for the Government to disseminate details of a child's health and education records to 400,000 public sector staff, even if most of the information has absolutely nothing to do with the child's welfare.

I know what it will mean. When my son was 10 my wife left him in the house for three minutes while she went out with my daughter to post a letter in the postbox 50 yards up the road. What she didn't realise was that a few minutes before she left the house our daughter had managed to dial 999. By the time my wife arrived back a policewoman was interrogating our son on what he was doing on his own in the house. A 10 year old left alone at home, she explained, is an emergency, on the same level as a missing toddler. (Never mind that school transport policy expects seven year olds to walk two miles to school along main roads.) Thanks to my wife's intervention, the police helicopters were called off, but, just to be sure, the next day, a social worker called at our house to conduct her own investigation. A tiny bit of common sense ought to have been enough to reassure the police and social services that there was nothing amiss. But common sense, unfortunately, is not a notable attribute of databases. It is pretty obvious what will happen with the

Children's Index: it will rapidly be overwhelmed with trivial and irrelevant information – and children in genuine peril will be overlooked.

If the Government needs a database on anything it is a database on its own databases. A cursory inspection would reveal what an appalling record it has when it comes to collecting data. Before they contemplate any more data collection enterprises ministers would be able to study such triumphs as the Department of Work and Pension's £412.5 million computer system, which crashed in November 2004, bringing chaos to the benefits system, and Connecting for Health, the NHS's new super computer system which has so far swallowed £6.5 billion in taxpayers' money, and has yet to show anything in return. One small part of the new system is Choose and Book, which is supposed to allow doctors to book their patients' hospital appointments online, at a hospital of the patient's choice. By 2004 Choose and Book was supposed to be handling 205,000 appointments a year. In fact it handled just 63. The following year that rose to 60,000 appointments, but mostly because the Government bribed GP practices to the tune of £100,000 each to use the system. How many of those 60,000 appointments were really made using the faltering system, and how many were actually made by telephone but recorded as being made online in order to claim the Government cash, is anyone's guess.

And just to cap it all…

While denying that the Children's Index amounts to a gross invasion of parents' and childrens' privacy, ministers have moved to make sure that their own children's health and education records will not have to be made available to all and sundry: children of celebrities and other well-known figures, it transpires, will be exempt from having to appear on the register.

17

THEY SAY
THEY'RE TRYING

L ET nobody say that the Government is blind to the problem of red tape. Even according to its own figures, lunatic regulations are costing British business one per cent of GDP every year, and it is trying to do something about them.

Spare a thought, then, for the poor civil servants trying, Canute-like, to repel the tide of incoming regulation. They can't get anywhere, it seems, without running into – well, red tape.

In 2001 the Government came up with the idea of Regulatory Reform Orders. These would enable a quango called the Better Regulation Taskforce to crackdown on unnecessary bureaucracy by issuing Government departments with orders to abolish those regulations and free businesses to get on with real work, rather than filling in forms. In 2005, however, the Government had an admission to make. Sorry, but Regulatory Reform Orders had turned out themselves to be 'complex and burdensome'. In four years the Better Regulation Taskforce had managed to issue orders cancelling a mere 27 regulations (a pitiful number against the 3,621 new regulations introduced in the 12 months to 31 May 2006). Designed as a rapid response unit, the taskforce was revealed to have taken more than eight months to issue each Regulatory Reform Order.

The solution? Among the big changes announced by the Government was the renaming of the 'Better Regulation Taskforce': it will now be known as the Better Regulation Commission. Wow! That's a change for the better. But this is not all. The Regulatory Impact Unit will henceforth be renamed the Better Regulation Executive – the fourth time it has been renamed in nine years.

In 2006 the Government announced yet another crackdown on red tape. It unveiled the Legislative and Regulatory Reform Bill which, it claimed, was all about making it easier to repeal regulations. What, in fact, the bill appeared to do was to make it easier for the Government to amend any law or regulation without having to go through the tiresome process of obtaining Parliament's approval. In other words, the 'red tape' which it wanted to tackle in reality consisted of the parliamentary regulations preventing governments from introducing laws at whim.

The Better Regulation Taskforce has another little achievement to its name: making life a little easier for the

Labour party's treasurers. Among a handful of regulations earmarked for scrapping in the taskforce's 69 page report, 'Less is More' is a rule which obliges trade unions to hold ballots of their members at least every 10 years to decide whether to continue handing over some of their money to political parties. How very convenient. Just the one question: in its great 'battle' against red tape does the Government intend to tackle any rules and regulations which make life difficult – and in one or two cases impossible – for the rest of us?

And just to assure you I am not being partisan here, the last Conservative Government had just as miserable a record when it came to deregulation. As trade minister (or President of the Board of Trade as he liked to call himself) in the early 1990s Michael Heseltine promised a 'bonfire of red tape'. The result? One or two rule changes making it easier for the Government to push through its road-building programme against local opposition.

One small law the Conservatives really did manage to repeal was the law insisting that all new bicycles be equipped with bicycle bells. Cyclists could always shout if there was someone in their way, ministers assured. Alas, no longer. In the latest transport act the Government introduced a new law to improve bicycle safety – an insistence that all cycles be fitted with a bell.

Although it has failed miserably to reduce the bureaucratic burden for business, the Government has at least attempted to help small businesses better understand the regulations to which they are obliged to genuflect. It set up the Small Business Service (SBS), a quango which maintains an interactive website, www.businesslink.gov.uk. The website itself cost £9 million – a princely sum, you might think, but a drop in the ocean compared with the total £404 million annual budget of the SBS. £147 million of this amount was spent on 'social enterprises', which are really job-creation schemes for the disadvantaged.

As an example of its work in this field the SBS has also funded a social enterprise called BizFizz, which boasts that it "has no rules, no set systems, no boundaries". What does this mean in practice? One client, it reports, "wanted to drive a taxi, but was known to be a heavy-drinker. This is a delicate personal issue that would fundamentally affect the success of his new business in a very small community which was aware of his drinking habits. The coach helped the client work through how others in the community would perceive his business idea and himself. The client then took the decision to change his drinking habits, and is now running a two-car taxi venture in partnership with his wife".

Presumably the SBS will next be helping kleptomaniacs to realise their dreams of opening banks and rapists to set up in business as escort agencies.

Here is one thing we could learn from Europe…
The Dutch have evolved a principle governing legislation: it is called 'one in, one out'. In other words if the Government makes a new regulation it must find an old regulation to repeal. Had that principle been in place in Britain over the past year it would have meant that 3,621 regulations would have been consigned to history.

Anyone have any suggestions for those which should go?

18

SOME BEDTIME

READING...

So you're hooked. Can't wait to curl up in bed with the Government's latest tome of rules and regulations? There is certainly no shortage of entertainment for the avid reader. In fact, there is something for all tastes.

On 1 June 2005, at the instigation of a Government beginning to get just a little concerned about the quantity of bureaucracy which it imposes upon its citizens, the accountants KPMG measured the burden of tax regulation on business. They concluded that conforming to tax rules laid down by Her Majesty's Revenue and Customs costs British business an astonishing £5.1 billion a year. That does not include the time individuals spend attending to their personal tax affairs, nor the cost of conforming to any regulation other than that concerning taxation.

In response the Government promised a blitz on red tape, freeing the citizen at last from the shackles of over-zealous officials. Well, up to a point. Over the following 12 months the Government introduced 29 acts of parliament and 3,592 statutory instruments – a total, with explanatory notes, of nearly 100,000 pages. Keen regulation-watchers will no doubt wish to read it all, which they can do on the Office of Public Sector Information website, www.opsi.gov.uk. For the benefit of the rest of you – i.e. anyone with hobbies or friends – I have produced some edited highlights of the new laws, regulations and other documents which will be shaping our lives.

1 November: The Bus Lane Contraventions (Penalty Charges, Adjudication and Enforcement) (England) Regulations 2005 come into force, laying down the rules for catching motorists who drive in bus lanes

Regulations ....23 pages

Explanatory notes ....4 pages

11 January: Food Hygiene (England) Regulations 2006 come into force, replacing, the Food Hygiene (England) Regulations 2005. Among the measures proposed are the reclassification of egg packing sheds. Henceforth they are no longer regarded as places of 'primary production', bringing them under a different regulatory regime.

The regulations ....42 pages

Explanatory notes ....84 pages

16 February: Equality Act becomes law, establishing a new quango, the Commission for Equality and Human Rights. It will also make it illegal to discriminate in the provision of goods and services on the basis of religion or sexual orientation. In other words are you a devil-worshipper who wants to be buried in a Church of England graveyard? No problem.

The Act itself ....90 pages

Explanatory notes ....46 pages

Racial and Religious Hatred Act 2006 also comes into force, introducing seven year jail sentences for those convicted of racial or religious hatred.

The Act itself .... 10 pages

Explanatory notes ....4 pages

Terrorism Act 2006 reaches the statute book, making it an offence, among other things, to glorify terrorism – or at least recent terrorism.

A time limit has avoided the possibility of the Archbishop of Canterbury being banged up for preaching on Samson's bringing down of the temple.

The Act itself ....47 pages

Explanatory notes ....36 pages

17 February: The Non-road mobile machinery (emission of gaseous and particulates pollutants) (amendment) Regulations 2006 come into force. Bundle of measures to cut the pong from lawn mowers.

The regulations ....19 pages

Explanatory notes ....28 pages

20 February: Department for Rural Affairs publishes Environment Permit Review, one of the department's 'flagship better regulation initiatives to slash red tape' ....92 pages

27 February: Her Majesty's Revenue and Customs publish a draft Income Tax Bill, part of the Tax Law Rewrite Project aimed at 'modernising UK direct tax law so that it is

clearer and easier to understand'.

Draft bill..798 pages

Draft Explanatory Notes (2 volumes) ....458 pages and 201 pages

"table of origins"................................320 pages

Women and Work Commission publish report 'Shaping a Fairer Future', proposing legislation to improve women's prospects in the workplace......................................148 pages

Department of Transport introduces new rules concerning children's seat belts..............

....18 pages

28 February: Health and Safety Commission publishes its Construction (Design and Management) Regulations, to 'simplify the regulations to improve clarity and make it easier for everyone to know what is expected of them'. ....177 pages

DTI publishes its draft consultation paper on 'strategic reference framework' – which governs the manner in which EU cash is splurged around the country ....99 pages

Consultation on policy for the long term management of solid low-level radioactive waste...74 pages

Employment Equality (Age) Regulations 2006 come into effect, making it an offence to discriminate against people in the workforce on the basis of age. (Not that the Government seems to feel the rules should apply to itself – it has decreed that public sector workers may continue to retire at 60, while private sector workers must go on to 68 before being allowed the state pension).

The regulations themselves ....53 pages

Guidance on how the regulations will affect pension schemes ....39 pages

Cabinet Office publishes a paper called Cutting Bureaucracy to Enable First Class Delivery of Local Government Services ....

....79 pages

27 March: Consultation on the Pharmacists and Pharmacy Technicians Order 2006 bringing pharmacy technicians under statutory regulation ....114 pages

29 March Consultation paper on UK ship recycling strategy published..............81 pages

Regulations published for new fee structure for local authorities to recoup from business the costs of regulating industrial plant...........

....90 pages

Consultation paper published on proposed Marine Bill, which invites interested parties to come up with suggestions for new ways to regulate all manner of activities related to the coast and sea................................270 pages

Defra publishes its 'Climate Change Programme' detailing suggested approaches to combating global warming.........202 pages

30 March Hurrah! It is one of the biggest days

of the regulation calendar. For a start, the Natural Environment and Rural Communities Bill receives royal assent. The main aim of the bill is to abolish a quango called English Nature – and replace it with one called . . . Natural England. There are a number of minor changes to the legislation protecting endangered species, though sadly this does not appear to include trees, as the bill runs to 113 pages and accompanying explanatory notes..42 pages

That's not all. The Consumer Credit Bill also receives royal assent, putting new restrictions on those who sell credit, and giving consumers the right to fight unfair credit agreements in the courts.

The bill itself... 74 pages
Explanatory notes ....32 pages

Also receiving royal assent today:

The Criminal Defence Services Bill, laying down new rules for when those charged with criminal offences can and cannot claim legal aid.

Framework document.......................... 22 pages

Supplement to Framework Document.............

....34 pages

Council Tax (New Valuation Lists for England) Act 2006, giving the Government the right to decide when our homes need revaluing for council tax purposes.

The bill..2 pages

Explanatory notes ....3 pages

Merchant Shipping (Pollution) Act 2006, which establishes an international regime for compensation for oil leaks from tankers.

The bill..3 pages

Explanatory notes ....8 pages

National Insurance Contributions Act 2006, making it easier for the Treasury to make retrospective changes in tax law......16 pages

Immigration, Asylum and Nationality Bill, supposedly tightens the law on illegal immigrants, but probably not in practice. A few weeks later the Home Office admits that it has lost track of a thousand foreign murderers, rapists and other criminals who have been released from jail and should have been deported.

The bill itself...41 pages

Explanatory notes.................................30 pages

And of course, the Identity Cards Bill, setting up a national identity cards register and paving the way to obliging all of us to carry ID cards, just in case we forget who we are. A big step forward for amnesiacs.

The bill itself.. 47 pages

Explanatory notes................................. 30 pages

4 April: The Sheep and Goats (Records, Identification and Movement) (Wales) Order 2006 ....45 pages

6 April: "A" day, the great moment when the Government's new rules for "Pensions Simplification" come into effect – supposedly replacing a complex web of rules and regulations with one simple regime as to who when and how an individual or a company may set up a pensions scheme. Any 20 year old minded to read the new regulations may well be retired by the time he finishes: the Registered Pension Schemes Manual runs to ....1,369 pages

6 April: But that is not all the fun and games. The first day of the new tax year also sees the Control of Noise at Work Regulations (2005) come into effect, laying down rules on how long workers can be allowed to work in a noisy environment.

Guidance notes ....19 pages
EC Directive ....7 pages

Regulatory Impact Assessment ....28 pages

6 April: Offshore Installations (safety case) Regulations 2005 come into effect, which are supposed to 'cut bureaucracy for industry and allow Health and Safety Executive inspectors to carry out more planned interventions' ....52 pages

6 April: Clean Neighbourhoods and Environment Act comes into force, making new regulations, among other things, as to where and where not you may allow your dog to pee, and laying down in remarkable detail the procedures which local authorities must follow before they may recover an abandoned shopping trolley from private land (and then how long they must keep the trolley for collection by the supermarket which owns it before being free to dispose of it).

The act itself..157 pages
Accompanying guidance notes.......350 pages
Further guidance notes for parish councils,

giving them powers to impose on-the-spot fines for louts ....116 pages

7 April: Gangmasters Licensing Authority comes into being, obliging the suppliers of casual labour to farms to obtain a licence for the first time. The new regulations are explained in three separate booklets, measuring a total of .... 49 pages In addition, there is a 'regulatory impact assessment' ....27 pages Plus a consultation on plans to extend similar measures to gangmasters supplying labour for the shellfish trade............................10 pages

7 April: Department of Constitutional Affairs publishes consultation on Burial Law and Policy in the 21st century, proposing rules on how crematoria use space – such as by stacking two corpses in one grave. ....37 pages

7 April: Treasury publishes second (corrected) version of the Finance Bill, explaining all the

tax changes and other measures in the budget (Gawd help those who ploughed through the first version). It comes in two volumes, weighing in at....................501 pages

12 April: Consultation paper published on changes to the Blood Safety and Quality Regulations...14 pages

27 April: Consultation on Legislative and Regulatory Reform Bill, the aim of which is 'to deliver reductions in unnecessary red tape by reducing or removing burdens, specifically financial costs, administrative burdens and distractions to efficiency, productivity and profitablity'.

Bill ....10 pages

Consultation document ....49 pages

27 April: Health and Safety Executive publishes consultation on how to force businesses to involve workers and trade unions more fully in health and safety issues. ....58 pages

4 May: Department of Health publishes its own 'simplification' plan ....30 pages

8 May: Defra publishes consultation on proposed changes to the law under the EU Habitats directive. This would oblige anyone undertaking extraction of water first to complete an environmental impact assessment...64 pages

8 May: Defra publishes consultation on welfare of animals during transport. The proposed regulations, which the UK is obliged to introduce under European directive EC 1/05, obliges anyone planning to transport a vertebrate more than 65 km to seek specific permission.

Consultation document ....75 pages
Accompanying EC directive...............44 pages

Planning for Tourism – new guidance notes for councils considering planning applications for leisure facilities................................49 pages

15 May: The Waste Management (England and Wales) Regulations 2006 come into effect, making it illegal for farmers to burn or otherwise dispose of waste on their farms with a license or exemption to do so. Unfortunately, in spite of the copious documents which farmers must now read to ensure they keep on the right side of the law the Government admits there is still 'no definitive list of what is and what is not waste' – leaving farmers perplexed as to whether they need permission to set up a dung pile or abandon a straw bale.

Consultation document .... 140 pages

Brochure of 'frequently-asked questions' .... 29 pages

24 May: Draft Legal Services Bill published .. .. 334 pages

25 May: Consumer Credit Act 2006 comes into force .... 74 pages

27 May: Consultation published on whether

to introduce pictoral health warnings alongside written health warnings on cigarette packets ....44 pages

19

A FEW

ABSURDITIES

TO FINISH...

Do not throw stones at this sign
Sole message spotted on a sign in the Republic of Ireland

WHEN I was an undergraduate at Cambridge in the 1980s I occasionally visited friends at Newnham, a ladies' college. The college once had a rule that if a gentleman was visiting a lady in her rooms the bed – a deliberately narrow 2ft 6 inch affair – must be wheeled into the corridor. By the time I arrived this rule had been relaxed, but had been replaced by one far more bizarre. Twenty years on I still occasionally scratch my head and try to work out the logic. At midnight, the main  doors to the college were locked, after which time the porters made sure that only members of the college could enter. Fair enough. But the porters were also there to ensure that no male was allowed to leave the college – unless he had a note from the female whom he had been visiting. Reach the front door after midnight without a note, and one was forbidden to exit. The only option then was to spend the entire night prowling the corridors – a situation which was not exactly conducive to the propriety which the rule was supposed to enforce.

I never found out who made up this rule, but circumstantial evidence leads me to conclude they are probably now working for the Department of Trade and Industry. Besides the puritanical, the archaic and pedantic, there are some rules and regulations which, however you look at them, simply don't make any sense at all.

There used to be just one body charged with ensuring fair competition: the Monopolies and Mergers Commission. Clearly, this opened the Government to charges of double standards: how can a quango devoted to fair competition be allowed to operate without any competition itself. So now there are three separate agencies working on the task: The Competition Commission, the Office of Fair Trading (OFT) and the Competition Appeal Tribunal. No-one can accuse them of being idle. The OFT handed out fines for price-fixing to, among others, Umbro, the sportswear manufacturer, and Hasbro, the manufacturers – ironically – of the board game Monopoly. Both companies were fined in spite of the fact that they hardly have a monopoly of their markets: they are in open competition with other sportswear manufacturers and games-makers. At the same time the

Government jealously guards near-monopolies of its own in education and health, and has gone out of its way to create monopolies in favoured industries. If you want to travel by train from London to Manchester you have a choice of just one train company, Virgin, which over the past ten years has doubled the standard open return fare to over £200.

When asked why the Government allowed train companies to exploit their monopolies by setting such high prices, former transport minister Lord Macdonald had a very helpful suggestion: why don't passengers travel by car instead?

The collapse of company pension funds in recent years has cost 85,000 people their pensions. In order to help these people – or at least theoretically in order to help these people – the Government in 2004 set up something called the Financial Assistance Scheme. In its first two years of operation the scheme had managed to compensate just 32 people, paying them an average of £3,125 each. Yet over the same period the scheme had itself cost £5 million to run. Needless to say, the civil servants who ran the scheme had no reason to worry about their pensions: they are assured a comfortable old age on an index-linked pension, calculated according to their final salary.

Such a privileged arrangement still fails to please many civil servants. On 28 March 2006, 1.5 million local authority staff went on strike to protest about plans to raise their retirement age from 60 to 65. Among the installations where staff walked out was the Thames Barrier. The Greater London Authority was, however, keen to reassure the public that staff would be on duty to provide 'emergency cover'. But what else is the Thames Barrier, an emergency flood defence, supposed to be for?

In 2005 the Advertising Standards Authority introduced a new set of regulations controlling the advertising of alcoholic drinks. Some of the rules one could understand. For example, it is now against the law to advertise beer in such a way as to suggest that boozing improves one's sexual performance or attraction to the opposite sex. Yet bizarrely, it is no longer possible to produce an advert which depicts alcoholic drink as making drinkers more aggressive, or even to suggest that drinking alters one's mood in any way. If alcohol did not alter the mood of the drinker it would not, of course, be necessary to regulate its sale at all. It is only because alcohol makes drinkers more aggressive, foolhardy or depressed that makes it a dangerous substance.

The ban does have a somewhat unintended consequence: it would now appear to be impossible to make an advert discouraging people from drinking too much by depicting anyone coming to grief while drunk.

So at least we're spared something.

And just to cheer you up, it could have been worse: a few nutty rules and regulations which might have been introduced – but haven't yet been:

• Plaid Cymru MP for Ceredigion, Simon Thomas, tried to pass the Organic Food and Farming Targets Bill, which would have forced British farmers, by 1 January 2010, to make sure that one third of all farming land was organic, and obliged shops to make sure that one fifth of all the food they sold was organic. Fortunately, the bill was rejected before we were all forced to live on carrots at £5 a time.

• Katarina Tomasevski, the UN Commission on Human Rights' 'special rapporteur on education' demanded that school exams be banned on the grounds that they breach Article 29 of the Human Rights convention, which demands education to be "directed to the development of the child's personality, talents and mental and physical abilities to their fullest potential".

• Seemingly unable to understand the concept of fun, Test Valley District Council in Hampshire suggested that householders cease having bonfires on 5 November and could instead have just as much fun putting the materials into a garden composter instead. Fortunately the council lacked the powers to impose an actual ban on bonfires.

Maybe it would have made a change for everyone to stand around munching hotdogs and watching Guy Fawkes being composted, but strangely I don't think it would serve as so severe a warning to would-be traitors.

20

CONCLUSION

ON that happy note, let's end this book here, before it grows to the length of a Government discussion document on the constitution of sheep worming-fluid. This has, necessarily, been a brief dip into the world of absurd rules and regulations. There is plenty more to be written on the finer points of the Climate Change and Sustainable Energy Act and the Waveney, Lower Yare and Lothingland Internal Drainage Board Order 2006. But we can leave that for another day.

My point is not that the world can get by without regulations. Clearly, there must be rules. Some things have to be registered and licensed, and beans must sometimes be counted. Yet the desire to regulate has reached the point at which it is beyond reason. Regulation has become an industry in itself, its practitioners judging their success by how much regulation they can produce. Unlike most other industries, this is not one which makes us richer. On the contrary, it is a parasite breeding upon those parts of the economy which are productive. Every time you fill in a form, undertake some complex 'assessment', apply for a licence to do something which you have been doing harmlessly for several years, you end up with less time to spend on productive work: it is as simple as that.

It is depressing that our political leaders and the civil servants who serve them cannot seem to see this. One detects in their wide-eyed fervour that they really believe that every time they dream up a new set of regulations they are making the world a better place. Theirs is a fantasy world. What in practice they are doing is simply forcing jobs and business overseas, to more lightly-regulated environments. Take the Religious Discrimination Laws. Companies must now lean over backwards to learn the date of every possible religious festival and its significance to the followers of that religion. Failure to do so can result in punitive awards for discrimination.

Does it benefit, say, Hindus? It certainly does. Not the Hindus working in Birmingham but the Hindus working in Mumbai, to where large parts of our service industries have vanished in recent years. The Government is unworried. Employment, repeats the Chancellor of the Exchequer, Gordon Brown, ad nauseam, has never been higher. Yet so many of the jobs created in Britain over the past decade –

650,000 of them to be precise – have been in areas of the public sector concerned with regulation; in other words they are in the business of making life more difficult for wealth-creators. It is a vicious circle: over-regulation forces industry to shed jobs; the surplus employees then get mopped up by Government and its quangos – dreaming up regulations which make life even more difficult for business.

Yet, as we have seen, so often when there is a clear case for a simple regulation the Government never gets round to doing anything. And even more disgracefully ministers have so often sought to exempt themselves from the rules which they impose upon others. Periodic attempts to cut red tape have been farcical, ending with the odd initiative to make life easier for the Government to push through its programme in the face of opposition: cutting out public inquiries, or simply ignoring them, but leaving the burden on business and individuals undiminished.

Raising eyebrows by taking a holiday almost immediately after taking office as 40th President of the United States in 1981, the late Ronald Reagan reminded critics that the country had voted for less Government and that was exactly what it was going to get. That is a spirit we could do with in our leaders today. Perhaps our only hope is that the working time regulations will eventually catch up with politicians so that by the time they have paraded around the country shaking hands and kissing babies they will have used up their statutory working hours and will have no time left available to spend concocting yet more regulation.

What a miserable, puritanical attitude it was that demanded John Prescott's head for being photographed playing croquet at his official residence, Dorneywood, on a working day. That was the least harmful thing he had done in office. To finish with a message for our leaders: lift your croquet mallets, the lot of you, and fight it out on the lawns of your official residence. And for goodness sake leave the rest of us alone.

QUESTIONNAIRE

**Under the Book (compulsory registration of data)
Regulations (2006)* readers of this book are
obliged to supply the following information.
Please fill in the form and return it to:**

Book Registration Data Collection Agency
Tessa Jowell House
Fyling Lane
Prescott New Town
East Tyneside
NE105 3PQ

Failure to complete this form may result in a fine not
exceeding £5,000

Book: How to Label a Goat, by Ross Clark

Your name:
_____

Date of birth:
_____

National Insurance number:
_____

Reading age (in years):
_____

Where did you obtain this book?

☐ a. Bookshop
☐ b. Internet
☐ c. Given it by a friend
☐ d. Other

Where did you read it?

☐ a. At home
☐ b. At work
☐ c. On train
☐ d. On beach
☐ e. On aeroplane
☐ f. Other (please specify)

_____

If you answered (e.) could you please also fill in your meal selection:

☐ Vegetarian
☐ Kosher
☐ Halal

How did you rate this book?

☐ a. Excellent
☐ b. Good
☐ c. Quite good
☐ d. Fairly good
☐ e. Satisfactory
☐ f. Fairly satisfactory
☐ g. Quite satisfactory
☐ h. Neither fairly satisfactory nor quite satisfactory
☐ i. Poor
☐ j. Very poor
☐ k. Extremely poor
☐ l. About as well written as the Sheep and Goats (Records, Identification and Movement) (Wales) Order 2006

QUESTIONNAIRE

Which pages did you enjoy most, in order?

_____

Did you use any of the following to help you read it?

☐ a. Spectacles
☐ b. Contact lens
☐ c. Monocle
☐ d. Pince-nez
☐ e. Other (please specify)

Please write down the names and titles of all other books you have read, since 11: (you may attach extra sheets of paper if you need to do·so)

_____

_____

What is the distance between your left and right ear lobes (in mm):

_____

How many bathrooms does your normal place of residence have?

_____

What do you intend to do with this book now?

☐ a. Keep it on bookshelf and read it again
☐ b. Give it to a friend
☐ c. Bin it
☐ d. Recycle it

☐ e. Keep it on bookshelf and never pick it up again
☐ f. If so, what height above the ground is the
    bookshelf, in feet and inches?

(If the answer to the last question is more than two
metres, please be aware of the requirements of the
EU Working at Heights Directive. Ring the helpline
for a leaflet on how to sue yourself)

To which ethnic group do you belong?

☐ a. White European
☐ b. Black European
☐ c. Mixed European
☐ d. White African (with sugar)
☐ e. White African (without sugar)
☐ f. Black African
☐ g. White and Black African
☐ h. Coloured African
☐ i. Coloured (short spin only)
☐ j. White (heavily soiled with pre-wash)

Please contact the Book Data Registration Collection
Agency for the remaining 190 pages of this form.